Miriam B. Loo's

Menu Planner Cookbook

Recipes Compiled by Miriam B. Loo

This book is dedicated to those people whom I've had the greatest pleasure of all entertaining — my husband, Orin, my three sons, Lester (Dusty), Gary and Roger (Skip), and their wonderful families.

Illustrated by
Dick Dahlquist and Marsha K. Howe

Dick Dahlquist

CONTENTS

Dear Friend,

A delicious meal is one way of showing family and friends that they are special, and it is with this thought in mind that I have written the **Menu Planner Cookbook** for you.

I hope you will enjoy creating these meals for your family and guests as much as I have for mine. All of the menus have been planned to provide both good nutritional value and to present foods that compliment each other in taste, texture and appearance. I have also been very careful to plan menus with foods that are easily obtainable in supermarkets. You'll find most of the meals feature cook-ahead dishes so you will be free to enjoy your own party in a relaxed and casual manner, and still serve a fine dinner.

When putting on a dinner party use your imagination for table decorations. Color sets a real festive mood, and that is one more way I use to say "it's been a pleasure to prepare this for you . . . happy dining!"

Most of these menus can easily be adapted for daily fare, too. Your family will surely appreciate the extra effort on your part, and a surprise gourmet meal is always a fun way to treat the most special people of all.

The potpourri chapter is a smattering of recipes that I think are particularly good, and although they are not used in the menus, I wanted to pass them along to you.

Bon Appétit!

Miriam B. Loo

Miriam B. Loo

Cookies
CHIPS
M.K. Howe

Brunch Menus

Serves 12

FRUIT KABOBS • DEVILED EGG CASSEROLE • BAKED HAM
CHICKEN DRUMLETS • GRITS CASSEROLE
COFFEE CAKE

"I have served the Deviled Egg Casserole many times and people always ask for the recipe. As a matter of fact, the whole menu is a real winner. Grits are one of my favorite dishes."

CHICKEN DRUMLETS

"In many markets, these delectable little morsels of the chicken are available packed by themselves. They are the meaty part of the wing with the bony section removed. Allow about 2 or 3 per serving unless you have a young crowd, then you may require more drumlets."

24 to 36 drumlets
½ cup soy sauce
⅓ cup dry sherry
¼ cup frozen orange juice concentrate, thawed
¼ cup firmly packed brown sugar
1 clove garlic, minced
½ teaspoon ground ginger *or* 1 teaspoon fresh ginger, grated
3 drops Tabasco® pepper sauce
Flour, salt and pepper
4 cups vegetable oil for frying

Soak drumlets (approximately 2 hours) in marinade composed of the ingredients listed with the exception of flour, salt and pepper and oil for frying. Be sure all pieces of meat are covered and turn from time to time. Drain drumlets and let sit a few minutes, then dredge in flour, salt and pepper. Fry in deep fat until golden brown. Drain on paper towels and keep warm, or cool and reheat on cookie sheet in 325° oven just before serving.

GRITS CASSEROLE

1 quart milk
½ cup real butter
1¼ cups hominy grits (not quick cooking)
1 teaspoon salt
⅛ teaspoon white pepper
⅓ cup real butter, melted
1½ cups grated Gruyere cheese *or* Cheddar cheese
⅓ cup grated Parmesan cheese

Bring milk to boil. Add ½ cup butter cut in pieces. Stir in grits. Resume boiling and continue cooking, stirring constantly until consistency of cooked farina. Remove from heat, add seasonings, then beat on high speed with electric mixer until grits take on a creamy appearance (about 5 minutes). Pour into 13 x 9 x 2-inch buttered casserole and let set. Cut into rectangular pieces. (Up to this point, the casserole may be made a day ahead and refrigerated.) Pour the ⅓ cup melted butter over rectangles and sprinkle with mixture of grated cheeses.

At serving time, heat in 400° oven for 30 minutes or until heated through thoroughly. If desired, put under broiler to brown the top.

COFFEE CAKE

"It's so rich, it doesn't need to be buttered!"

½ cup chopped walnuts *or* pecans
¼ cup sugar
1 tablespoon ground cinnamon
1½ cups all-purpose flour
1 teaspoon baking powder
½ teaspoon baking soda
½ cup butter *or* margarine
1 cup sugar
2 eggs, well beaten
1 tablespoon vanilla
1 cup dairy sour cream

Combine chopped nuts with ¼ cup sugar and cinnamon. Set aside. Blend together flour, baking powder and soda. Cream butter or margarine with 1 cup sugar until light and fluffy. Add eggs and vanilla and beat well. Add dry ingredients and sour cream. Fold until well blended. Pour ½ the batter into greased and lightly floured 9-inch square pan. Top with ½ of the cinnamon-nut mixture. Cover with remaining batter and top with remaining cinnamon-nut mixture. Bake at 375° for 30 to 35 minutes or until golden brown.

Note: This light textured coffee cake can be made the day before. Serve hot or cold.

DEVILED EGG CASSEROLE

Stuffed eggs:
20 hard-cooked eggs,
cut in half lengthwise
½ cup mayonnaise
1 teaspoon dry mustard
½ teaspoon Worcestershire sauce
Salt and pepper to taste

Sauce:
⅔ cup butter *or* margarine
1 cup chopped celery
1 pound fresh mushrooms, sliced
3 cups milk
1 cup canned chicken broth
1 tablespoon instant onion
1 cup all-purpose flour
3 cups half-and-half
½ teaspoon salt *or* to taste
1⅓ cups sliced ripe olives
1½ cups fine bread stuffing
mixture
3 tablespoons butter *or* margarine,
melted

Remove yolks from hard-cooked eggs. Put whites aside. Mash yolks until free of lumps. Add remaining ingredients for stuffed eggs and mix until smooth. Refill egg whites with yolk mixture and set aside.

For sauce, melt ⅔ cup butter or margarine in large skillet and add celery. Sauté until tender but not brown; remove and reserve. Add sliced mushrooms to skillet and cook until tender; return celery to pan with mushrooms. In bowl, combine milk and chicken broth; add instant onion and stir in flour with whisk until well blended. Pour into skillet with celery-mushroom mixture. Cook over medium heat until thick and smooth, stirring constantly. Slowly add half-and-half, stirring until thoroughly heated. Add ½ teaspoon salt or salt to taste. Remove from heat and stir in ripe olives.

Pour a very thin layer of sauce in bottom of 2 large shallow casseroles (11¾ x 7½ x 1¾-inch). Arrange stuffed eggs on top of sauce; top with remaining sauce. Combine fine bread stuffing mixture with melted butter or margarine; sprinkle over top of egg dish. Bake at 350° for 20 minutes or until hot and bubbly.

Note: Do not overcook eggs. Additional baking in hot sauce will make them tough and rubbery. This recipe can be made a day before and refrigerated with exception of the addition of the bread stuffing, which should be added just prior to baking.

BAKED HAM

"Use your own favorite ham recipe or try this one which imparts an excellent flavor to the ham when cold."

1 medium onion, sliced
1 large carrot, sliced
1 tablespoon butter *or* margarine
1 tablespoon vegetable oil
3 fresh parsley sprigs
1 bay leaf
¼ teaspoon dried thyme
1 4- to 5-pound cooked ham, skinned and trimmed of excess fat
1½ cups canned beef broth
½ cup Madeira wine
⅓ cup confectioners' sugar

Preheat oven to 350°. Sauté the vegetables in butter or margarine and oil for about 10 minutes in a roasting pan or casserole, until they are very lightly browned. Add parsley, bay leaf and thyme. Place ham over vegetables, fat side up; add broth and wine and bring to simmer on top of stove. Cover and place roaster or casserole in middle of preheated oven. Regulate heat so that liquid barely simmers for about 1½ hours. Baste frequently with juices in pan.

Remove from oven and sprinkle confectioners' sugar over the top of the ham and return to oven under broiler. Watch closely until nice and evenly browned. Cool and refrigerate. When cold, slice very thinly and arrange attractively on platter for serving. Serve at room temperature.

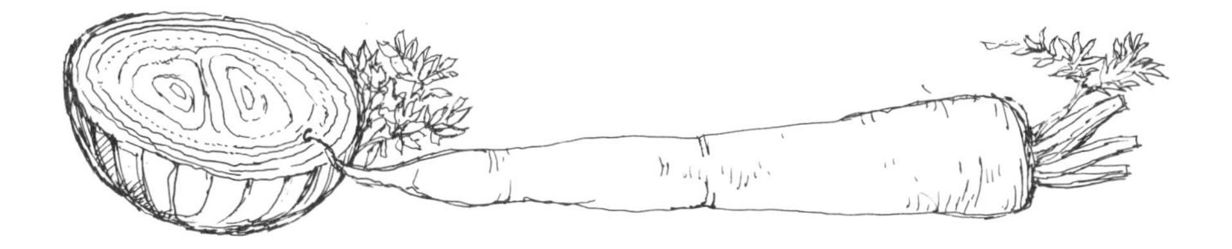

FRUIT KABOBS

1 6-ounce can frozen limeade, thawed
32 fresh whole strawberries
32 green seedless grapes, if available
32 fresh pineapple wedges *or* canned chunks
32 cantaloupe balls (use honeydew, watermelon or combination of the 3 as available)
16 bamboo sticks

Pour undiluted, thawed limeade over fruit in large bowl. Chill at least 2 hours. Alternate fruit on bamboo sticks. Serve with fruit dips if desired.

Note: Stick kabobs into melon half (cut side down) or arrange on platter for serving.

Lemon Dip: Combine 1⅓ cups dairy sour cream, ¼ cup confectioners' sugar and 1 teaspoon grated lemon peel. Makes: 1½ cups.

Pineapple Cream: Combine 1 cup dairy sour cream, ½ cup drained crushed pineapple, ⅓ cup chopped mixed nuts, 1 tablespoon maraschino cherry juice and ⅛ teaspoon ground ginger. Makes: 2 cups.

Cranberry Dip: Combine 1 16-ounce can jellied cranberry sauce, 1 teaspoon cider vinegar and ½ teaspoon dry mustard. Use electric mixer or blender to make smooth dip. Makes: 2 cups.

Note: If fresh fruit is out of season, substitute any combination of drained, canned fruit chunks such as pears, peaches, pitted dark sweet cherries and pineapple chunks.

Serves 8

TOMATO-BEEF BOUILLON • BAKED CHEESE FONDUE
BANANA PANCAKES • BACON or SAUSAGE
MINTED MELON SLICES

"This menu is an unusual combination but really good. If you're going to be serving youngsters, this is a particularly good choice."

TOMATO-BEEF BOUILLON

12 cups tomato juice
12 beef bouillon cubes
½ teaspoon onion salt
½ teaspoon celery salt
1 tablespoon sugar
¼ teaspoon garlic salt
5 drops Tabasco® pepper sauce
Salt to taste
1 tablespoon Worcestershire sauce
1 tablespoon fresh lemon juice
Thin peel of lemon

Place **1 cup** tomato juice in saucepan with bouillon cubes and bring to boil, stirring to dissolve cubes. Cool the juice and add to rest of ingredients with exception of lemon peel. Refrigerate and chill.

To each serving, add a thin twist of lemon peel for taste and color.

BANANA PANCAKES

2¼ cups all-purpose flour
4 teaspoons baking powder
2 tablespoons sugar
¾ teaspoon salt
3 eggs, well beaten
2 cups milk
4 tablespoons butter *or* margarine, melted
3 large or 4 small very ripe bananas, mashed
Butter *or* margarine, melted
Sugar

Sift together dry ingredients. In small bowl, combine eggs, milk, melted butter or margarine and add to dry ingredients. Stir until moistened. Add mashed bananas and stir. Bake on hot griddle or heavy fry pan with generous amount of butter or margarine. This will take about twice as long as a regular pancake to cook. Remove to warming plate. Serve with melted butter or margarine and sugar.

Note: This recipe will make about 16 4-inch cakes.

MINTED MELON SLICES

2 ripe cantaloupes *or* other type melon
Sprinkle of salt
2 tablespoons finely chopped fresh mint
Mint leaves for garnish

Peel melon and cut into 1-inch slices. Layer in bowl, sprinkling each layer with slightest bit of salt and sprinkling of finely chopped mint. Let marinate for a couple of hours in the refrigerator prior to serving. Garnish with mint leaves.

BAKED CHEESE FONDUE

14 ½-inch slices French bread cut from long narrow loaf
½ cup butter or margarine, softened
1 medium onion, coarsely grated
1 large carrot, coarsely grated
⅔ pound sharp Cheddar cheese, grated
1 teaspoon dried thyme
¼ cup chopped fresh parsley
2 teaspoons dried basil
5 eggs
2¾ cups milk
2 tablespoons Dijon mustard
1½ teaspoons Worcestershire sauce
½ teaspoon salt
¼ teaspoon paprika

Spread crusted bread slices with softened butter and cut into 1-inch-square cubes. Place ½ of the cubes in a 2-quart soufflé dish. Sprinkle with ½ of the onion, carrot and cheese plus ½ of the herb mixture of thyme, parsley and basil. Repeat layer of bread, followed by vegetables, cheese and herbs.

Beat together eggs, milk, mustard, Worcestershire sauce, salt and paprika. Pour over contents of soufflé dish and refrigerate, covered, overnight. Remove from refrigerator and let stand at room temprature for 45 minutes before baking at 350° for 1 hour.

Serves 6

MARINATED ARTICHOKE HEARTS
HAM AND EGGS AU GRATIN
CHICKEN LIVERS IN ONION-WINE SAUCE
CREAM CHEESE BISCUITS • SWEDISH FRUIT COMPOTE

"Easy to do ahead. The biscuits are a real surprise and a sure hit with the guests."

MARINATED ARTICHOKE HEARTS

2 9-ounce packages frozen artichoke hearts
½ cup vegetable oil *or* ¼ cup each, vegetable oil and olive oil
⅓ cup wine vinegar
2 tablespoons chopped fresh parsley
1 clove garlic, minced
3 or 4 drops Tabasco® pepper sauce
Lettuce, washed, dried, chilled

Cook artichoke hearts according to package directions. Drain well. Mix oil, wine vinegar, parsley, garlic and pepper sauce and pour over hot artichoke hearts. Toss carefully. Cool and refrigerate overnight, spooning marinade over once or twice. Serve on shredded lettuce leaves.

SWEDISH FRUIT COMPOTE

"A nice little garnish for this is to sprinkle about ½ cup toasted coconut flakes over the top."

- 1 11-ounce package mixed dried fruits
- ½ cup raisins
- ¾ of an inch stick of cinnamon
- 4 cups water
- 1 medium orange, unpeeled, halved and thinly sliced
- 1 18-ounce can pineapple juice (2¼ cups)
- ½ cup red currant jelly
- ¼ cup sugar
- 2 tablespoons quick cooking tapioca
- ¼ teaspoon salt

In large saucepan, combine mixed fruits, raisins, cinnamon and water. Bring to boil, simmer uncovered until fruits are tender, about 30 minutes. Add remaining ingredients, bring to boil, cover and cook over low heat 15 minutes longer, stirring occasionally. Remove stick cinnamon and serve warm or chilled in individual dishes, depending on the weather and your mood.

HAM AND EGGS AU GRATIN

- 4 tablespoons butter *or* margarine
- 4 tablespoons all-purpose flour
- 2 cups milk, scalded
- 1½ teaspoons prepared mustard
- 1½ teaspoons Worcestershire sauce
- 1 cup grated Cheddar cheese
- ½ pound cooked ham cut in ½-inch cubes
- 6 hard-cooked eggs, halved
- ⅔ cup fine bread crumbs
- 2 tablespoons butter *or* margarine, melted

In saucepan, melt 4 tablespoons butter or margarine, add flour and cook 2 minutes while stirring. Add milk, stirring constantly with whisk. Simmer until thickened. Add mustard, Worcestershire sauce and cheese and heat until cheese melts. Add ham and heat through.

Pour ½ the sauce into a flat baking dish. Arrange halved eggs on sauce. Cover with remaining sauce, then bread crumbs mixed with 2 tablespoons melted butter. (Up to this point, this may be prepared ahead of time and refrigerated.)

At serving time, heat until bubbly and hot in moderate oven. Don't overcook or eggs will become rubbery.

CHICKEN LIVERS IN ONION-WINE SAUCE

½ cup all-purpose flour
½ teaspoon salt
⅛ teaspoon freshly ground black pepper
1½ pounds chicken livers, cleaned and dried
4 tablespoons butter *or* margarine
½ cup finely minced scallions, some green part included
¼ cup finely minced fresh parsley
¼ teaspoon dried thyme
⅓ cup dry vermouth
Cherry tomatoes
Fresh parsley

Put flour, salt and pepper into small paper bag. Shake chicken livers in this mixture until well coated. (Add more flour, salt and pepper if needed to cover.) Heat butter or margarine in skillet until quite hot. Add chicken livers and cook for 3 or 4 minutes, turning to brown evenly. Remove from pan and keep warm. Sauté onions in the same skillet, adding a bit of butter or margarine if necessary. When onions are limp, add chicken livers and rest of ingredients except cherry tomatoes and parsley garnish. Cook another 3 or 4 minutes. Adjust seasoning. Take care not to overcook the chicken livers, as they will become tough.

Serve on a piece of dry toast for each individual serving. Garnish with halved cherry tomatoes and parsley.

CREAM CHEESE BISCUITS

"This recipe is easy to cut in half, but they're so delicious, you'll wish you'd made the whole batch."

2 cans refrigerated flaky biscuits (20 biscuits total)
½ cup granulated sugar
1 teaspoon ground cinnamon
¼ teaspoon ground cloves
¼ teaspoon ground nutmeg
¼ teaspoon ground allspice
6 tablespoons butter *or* margarine, melted
¾ cup chopped pecans
2 3-ounce packages cream cheese

Remove biscuits from 1 can and place them about 1 inch apart on board sprinkled with some sugar. With rolling pin, gently roll over them all at one time, in one direction then the other, until each biscuit is about 3 inches in diameter. In small bowl, mix sugar with spices. In each of 2 9-inch pie pans, pour 2 tablespoons melted butter or margarine; sprinkle 2 tablespoons sugar and spice mix and 3 tablespoons nuts.

Score 1 package cream cheese in tenths, by cutting in half the long way, then in 4 equally spaced cuts the short way. On each enlarged biscuit, place a piece of cream cheese and ½ teaspoon of the sugar mixture. Dampen outside edge with milk, fold over and carefully press down edges with tines of fork. In remaining 2 tablespoons butter or margarine, dip 1 side of each biscuit and place in pan buttered side up, forming a pinwheel. When all biscuits are buttered and placed in pan, sprinkle with 1 tablespoon of sugar mixture and ½ of the remaining nuts. Repeat procedure with remaining biscuits and ingredients, fitting biscuits into second prepared pan. Bake in 375° oven for 20 minutes until browned. The biscuits may be turned upside down on a serving dish.

Note: Biscuits may be prepared ahead, refrigerated then baked just before serving.

Serves 4

BROILED GRAPEFRUIT or BAKED STUFFED APPLES
SWEDISH PANCAKES
SAUSAGE AND BACON BROIL

"Our family's favorite – but maybe that is natural since we are of Scandinavian descent. That is, my husband is. I'm English, but I have learned to prepare and enjoy many Scandinavian foods."

BROILED GRAPEFRUIT

2 grapefruit
4 tablespoons concentrated orange juice, frozen
4 tablespoons firmly packed dark brown sugar
4 green *or* red maraschino cherries

Cut the grapefruit in half and section with grapefruit knife, removing center white part. Mix orange juice and dark brown sugar together. Spread ¼ of the mixture on each grapefruit half. Broil for about 10 minutes to melt sugar. Garnish with maraschino cherry in center of each half.

SWEDISH PANCAKES

"Mix batter and refrigerate overnight."

3 eggs
2 cups milk
1 cup all-purpose flour
1½ teaspoons granulated sugar
½ teaspoon salt
¼ cup butter *or* margarine, melted
Confectioners' *or* granulated sugar

Have all ingredients at room temperature. Blend first 5 ingredients until completely free of lumps. Blend in melted butter or margarine. Refrigerate. To bake, brush 7- or 8-inch skillet lightly with butter or margarine and heat over moderately high heat until small drops of water sizzle and dance on it. Pour 2 to 3 tablespoons batter into middle of pan, then tilt pan in all directions to cover bottom with thin film of batter. Cook for a couple of minutes, turn and cook about ½ minute on the other side (this side does not brown very well). Slide pancake onto plate and continue with batter. Stack pancakes as they are baked and keep warm in oven until ready to serve.

To serve: Spread pancakes with melted butter or margarine, sprinkle with confectioners' sugar or granulated sugar and roll. Or for another serving idea, sprinkle with sugar and spread with lingonberry preserves or cranberry jelly, roll and sprinkle with sugar again.

SAUSAGE AND BACON BROIL

½ pound hickory smoked bacon
½ pound brown-and-serve sausages

Put bacon on broiler pan and taking care not to burn, place under broiler until nearly done to your liking. Put brown-and-serve sausages on broiler pan and heat through while finishing cooking bacon. Drain on paper towels and serve.

BAKED STUFFED APPLES

4 golden delicious apples *or* other baking apples in season
4 tablespoons currants *or* raisins
4 tablespoons honey
½ teaspoon ground nutmeg
½ teaspoon ground cinnamon
3 tablespoons chunky peanut butter
1 tablespoon butter *or* margarine, softened

Remove stems and core apples, being certain all seeds and pockets are removed. Pare a thin area of skin from the blossom end of the apples. Set apples in an 8-inch baking pan. Mix together the currants or raisins, honey, nutmeg, cinnamon, peanut butter and softened butter or margarine and stuff each apple cavity. Add ¼ cup of water to bottom of pan. Bake in 375° oven for 20 to 30 minutes. Apples should be firm, not mushy. Serve with thick cream, if desired.

Luncheon Menus

Serves 8

CREPES CANNELLONI • SHRIMP AND CRAB CREPES
STUFFED CHICKEN CREPES
CUCUMBER MOUSSE
LEMON OR ORANGE SHERBET WITH CHOCOLATE SAUCE

"Select one or two kinds of crepes, two are plenty per serving. The light, delicate flavor of the Cucumber Mousse is especially good with the rest of the menu."

STUFFED CHICKEN CREPES

(See the basic crepe recipe included with French dinner menu on page 43 with the Crepes Frangipane.)

- 8 chicken thighs
- 3 tablespoons butter *or* margarine
- 1 chicken bouillon cube
- ½ cup boiling water
- 4 tablespoons all-purpose flour
- ½ teaspoon paprika
- ½ teaspoon salt
- Dash of pepper
- 1 cup half-and-half
- ½ pound fresh mushrooms, sliced
- 2 tablespoons butter *or* margarine
- ⅓ cup dry white wine
- 4 brown-and-serve sausage links, halved lengthwise
- 8 6-inch crepes

Brown the chicken thighs in 3 tablespoons butter or margarine. Dissolve bouillon cube in boiling water and add to chicken. Cover and simmer until tender, 20 to 30 minutes. Remove chicken (reserving broth), cool slightly, then carefully remove bone from chicken thigh, doing so from the under area. Skim fat from broth in which chicken was cooked and add enough water to make ¾ cup liquid. Return to skillet. Combine flour, paprika, ½ teaspoon salt and dash of pepper; blend in half-and-half. Add to broth, cook and stir until sauce is thickened and bubbly. Sauté mushrooms in 2 tablespoons butter or margarine until tender; add mushrooms and wine to the sauce.

To assemble the crepes, insert a sausage half in bone cavity of each chicken thigh; lay chicken in center of crepe on unbrowned side. Top with 1 tablespoon sauce. Fold two opposite edges so they overlap the chicken. Place seam side down in a buttered 12 x 7½ x 2-inch baking dish. Repeat with remaining crepes. Spoon rest of sauce over crepes. Cover and bake at 375° about 25 minutes, until heated through.

CREPES CANNELLONI

(See the basic crepe recipe included with French dinner menu on page 43 with the Crepes Frangipane.)

Cream sauce:
6 tablespoons butter *or* margarine
4 tablespoons all-purpose flour
⅛ teaspoon salt
Dash of white pepper
4 chicken bouillon cubes
1½ cups evaporated milk diluted with 1½ cups water, then scalded
½ cup grated Parmesan cheese

Filling:
¾ pound lean ground beef
¼ pound ground pork
Salt and pepper to taste
4 tablespoons butter *or* margarine
½ cup chopped onions
½ cup chopped fresh mushrooms
2 tablespoons tomato paste
1 egg
1½ cups grated Parmesan cheese
½ of a 10-ounce package frozen spinach, cooked and finely chopped
Dash ground nutmeg
Approximately 12 6-inch crepes

For cream sauce, melt butter or margarine in saucepan over low heat; blend in flour, salt, pepper and chicken bouillon cubes. Stir with whisk until bubbly but not browned. Add 1½ cups scalded milk and stir until thickened. (At this point, put aside ½ cup sauce for the meat filling and 1 tablespoon for the spinach.) To remainder of sauce, add rest of scalded milk and stir until thickened. Add the ½ cup grated cheese and remove from heat.

For filling, mix together beef and pork; season to taste, then sauté in 2 tablespoons butter or margarine until meat is cooked. Set aside. Sauté onions in remaining 2 tablespoons butter or margarine. Add mushrooms and tomato paste and continue to sauté until vegetables are limp. Return meat to skillet with vegetables. Add ½ cup cream sauce (before sauce is diluted with all of the milk — see sauce recipe), 1 egg, ½ cup grated cheese, and salt and pepper to taste to meat mixture. Thaw spinach and cook according to package directions. Drain well and chop finely. Dust with nutmeg, salt and pepper. Add 1 tablespoon reserved cream sauce (see sauce recipe above). Blend.

To assemble, spread each crepe down the center with 2 teaspoons spinach. Spread over this, 2 tablespoons of the meat mixture. Roll crepe and place seam side down in a buttered, shallow oven casserole. Continue until all ingredients are used. Cover crepes with the remaining cream sauce and sprinkle with 1 cup grated cheese.

Before serving, heat in 350° oven until bubbly and cheese is golden, about 20 to 30 minutes. You may put under broiler for 2 to 4 minutes to brown.

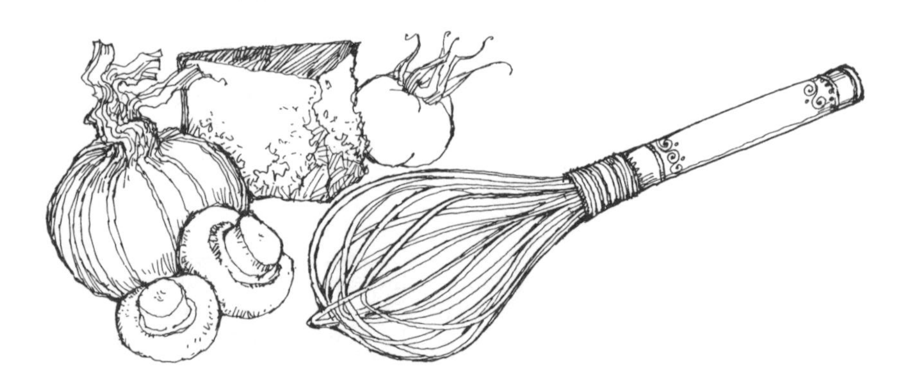

SHRIMP AND CRAB CREPES

(See the basic crepe recipe included with French dinner menu on page 43 with the Crepes Frangipane.)

¾ cup sliced fresh mushrooms
¼ cup finely chopped onion
¼ cup butter *or* margarine
¼ cup all-purpose flour
¼ teaspoon salt
1½ cups milk
1 7½-ounce can crab meat, drained, flaked and cartilage removed
1 6-ounce can shrimp *or* frozen tiny shrimp
3 tablespoons dry sherry
Salt, pepper and fresh lemon juice to taste
¾ cup grated Swiss *or* Gruyere cheese
Paprika
Approximately 12 6-inch crepes

Sauté mushrooms and onion in ¼ cup butter or margarine. Blend in flour and salt. Add milk and cook, stirring until thickened and bubbly. Gently stir in crab meat, shrimp and sherry. Taste for salt and pepper and possible squeeze of lemon juice. Remove from heat.

To assemble: On each crepe, spread about 2 tablespoons filling, roll and put seam side down in buttered baking dish in one layer. Heat about 15 to 20 minutes in 350° oven, then sprinkle grated cheese over the top and return to oven until cheese melts, about 10 minutes. Sprinkle lightly with paprika before serving.

CUCUMBER MOUSSE

1 3-ounce package lime-flavored gelatin
¾ cup boiling water
1 envelope unflavored gelatin
¼ cup cold water
1 cup mayonnaise
¼ medium onion, chopped
1 cup cottage cheese
1 peeled medium cucumber, chopped
⅛ teaspoon Tabasco® pepper sauce
1 medium clove garlic, minced
Green food coloring
Lettuce, washed, dried, and chilled

Dissolve lime-flavored gelatin in boiling water and add unflavored gelatin which has been softened in cold water. In blender, put the mayonnaise, onion, cottage cheese, cucumber, pepper sauce, garlic and blend until smooth. Add the 2 gelatins and blend again. Add a drop of green food coloring. Mold and chill overnight. Serve on crisp lettuce leaves.

LEMON OR ORANGE SHERBET WITH CHOCOLATE SAUCE

1 quart lemon *or* orange sherbet
½ cup flaked toasted coconut
½ cup chopped, toasted almonds

Chocolate sauce:
1 cup sugar
1 cup water
½ cup light corn syrup
3 1-ounce squares unsweetened chocolate, broken into bits
1 teaspoon vanilla
½ cup evaporated milk

For sauce, combine sugar, water and corn syrup and cook to soft ball stage (236°). Remove from heat. Add chocolate and stir until melted. Add vanilla, then slowly add evaporated milk and mix thoroughly. Cool. This makes 1¾ cups sauce.

To serve, put a slice or 2 scoops of sherbet on each plate. Over this, drizzle chocolate sauce, sprinkle with toasted coconut and then toasted almonds.

Serves 6

COLD AVOCADO SOUP • HOT CHICKEN SALAD
PICKLED VEGETABLES • SESAME SEED BREAD STIX
MASCARPONE WITH FRUIT

"I like this avocado soup recipe because you don't have to count on finding ripe avocados. The whole menu is easy to prepare ahead of time."

PICKLED VEGETABLES

¼ cup water
½ medium head cauliflower, broken into flowerlets
2 carrots, cut in 2-inch strips
2 celery ribs, cut in 1-inch pieces
1 small green pepper, cut in strips
¾ cup red wine vinegar
½ cup olive oil
1 tablespoon sugar
1 teaspoon salt
½ teaspoon dried basil
¼ teaspoon dried tarragon
1 cup pitted ripe olives

At least **2 hours** before serving or early in the day: In large skillet over medium heat, put ¼ cup water and heat all ingredients except olives to boiling, stirring occasionally. Reduce heat to low; simmer, covered, 3 to 5 minutes until vegetables are tender-crisp. Remove from heat and add olives. Chill, covered, for 1 hour. Drain well.

MASCARPONE WITH FRUIT

"Each serving has some cream and some fruit. A bite of the two together is delicious."

Mixture of fresh fruit, peeled and sliced, as necessary
1 6-ounce can frozen limeade
1 8-ounce and 1 3-ounce package of cream cheese, at room temperature
⅓ cup sifted confectioners' sugar
2 tablespoons half-and-half
3 tablespoons orange-flavored liqueur
1 tablespoon orange juice concentrate, thawed
1 tablespoon grated orange peel

Prepare fruit, such as sliced peaches, apricots, pears, strawberries, melon slices, blueberries and oranges. Marinate in limeade (to keep from discoloring) a couple of hours before serving time. If canned fruit is used, place canned halves of peaches, apricots, pears and pineapple in skillet with a little juice and sugar and sauté until glazed. Chill before serving.

In food processor or blender, blend together all other ingredients until smooth (should be consistency of sherbet). Arrange cream in the center of a serving plate and swirl into an attractive pattern. Surround with the drained fruit.

COLD AVOCADO SOUP

1 10½-ounce can chicken broth
1 7¾-ounce can frozen avocado dip, thawed
¼ cup water
1 tablespoon fresh lemon juice
1 cup dairy sour cream
3 slices bacon, finely chopped, fried crisp and drained
Fresh parsley

Combine chicken broth, avocado dip, water and lemon juice. Put in blender and blend until smooth. Stir in sour cream and chill. Serve in chilled bowls topped with bacon bits and garnish with a sprig of parsley.

HOT CHICKEN SALAD

2 cups diced cooked chicken
½ cup slivered toasted almonds
2 teaspoons grated onion
2 cups coarsely chopped celery
2 teaspoons fresh lemon juice
½ teaspoon salt
1 cup mayonnaise
½ cup grated Cheddar cheese
1 cup crushed potato chips

Combine chicken, almonds, onion, celery, lemon juice, salt and mayonnaise. Put into a shallow baking dish, sprinkle with grated cheese and crushed potato chips. Bake at 400° for about 20 minutes until bubbly.

Note: Put together ahead of time with exception of potato chips. Add crushed chip topping and bake just before serving.

Serves 6

CRAB QUICHE • BAKED STUFFED TOMATOES
HOT ROLLS • LIME SHERBET WITH STRAWBERRIES

"Most everyone is impressed with a quiche, and this one is especially good because of the delicate flavor of the crab. The stuffing in the baked tomatoes is very tasty."

CRAB QUICHE

Pastry:
1½ cups all-purpose flour
½ teaspoon salt
½ cup solid shortening
4 to 5 tablespoons cold water
1 egg white, beaten with a few grains of salt

Filling:
1 cup shredded Swiss cheese
1 7½-ounce can crab meat, drained, flaked and cartilage removed
2 green onions, sliced with tops
4 eggs, well beaten
1¼ cups half-and-half
½ teaspoon salt
1 teaspoon prepared mustard
½ teaspoon grated lemon rind
Dash of ground mace
¼ cup sliced toasted almonds

For pastry, sift flour and salt; cut in shortening until pieces are the size of small peas. Sprinkle with water, 1 tablespoon at a time, tossing with fork until water is absorbed. Form into a ball, flatten on lightly floured board and roll to ¼-inch thick. Place in 10-inch pie pan, shape edges, prick lightly and brush with beaten egg white.

Note: Refrigerate for ½ hour before filling.

To fill the pastry shell, first sprinkle with cheese. Top with crab meat and sprinkle with onion. In a medium-size bowl, combine eggs, half-and-half, salt, mustard, lemon rind and mace; beat well. Pour over crab meat and top with sliced almonds. Bake at 325° for 45 minutes or until set. Remove from oven and let stand 10 minutes before serving.

LIME SHERBET WITH STRAWBERRIES

"A simple, refreshing little taste of sweet to finish the meal."

1 pint lime sherbet
1 quart strawberries, washed, hulled and halved, reserving 6 beauties to put atop each serving
Sugar added to berries to taste

Surround a rather large scoop of lime sherbet with sliced and sweetened berries. Top scoop of sherbet with a perfect strawberry.

BAKED STUFFED TOMATOES

6 medium tomatoes
⅓ cup finely chopped green pepper
⅓ cup finely chopped green onion
⅓ cup finely chopped celery
2 tablespoons butter *or* margarine
16 soda crackers, rolled into fine crumbs
Salt and pepper to taste
Grated Parmesan cheese
Paprika

Scald tomatoes, peel and scoop out inside leaving a thick shell. Turn upside down to drain. Chop removed pulp and set aside. Sauté green pepper, green onion and celery in butter or margarine until tender but not browned. Add reserved tomato pulp and cracker crumbs. Add salt and pepper to taste.

Fill tomatoes with mixture. Sprinkle with Parmesan cheese and paprika. Dot with butter or margarine. Bake at 400° for 20 to 25 minutes.

Serves 8

CHICKEN SALAD WITH GARNISH
CINNAMON BISCUITS • RASPBERRY BISCUITS
MACAROON TORTONI WITH STRAWBERRIES

"Chicken salad is an old favorite of mine. Use your imagination with the garnish to make a really pretty plate. The tortoni is a delicious dessert that you can make up to a week ahead of time if you wish."

CHICKEN SALAD WITH GARNISH

"Another serving suggestion, instead of the vegetable, egg garnish – use fresh fruit, such as melon, pineapple chunks and orange sections."

4 cups diced cooked chicken breasts
2 cups coarsely chopped celery
2 tablespoons fresh lemon juice
1 cup slivered toasted almonds
1½ teaspoons salt
½ teaspoon pepper
1½ cups seedless green grapes (optional)*
¾ cup heavy cream, whipped
1½ cups mayonnaise
Lettuce, washed, dried and chilled
Hard-cooked eggs, tomatoes and pitted ripe olives

Combine chicken, celery, lemon juice, almonds, salt, pepper and grapes (optional). Toss and refrigerate for at least 1 hour or until well chilled. Just before serving, whip cream, fold into mayonnaise, then fold into chicken mixture. Serve chicken on a bed of lettuce garnished with quartered hard-cooked eggs, tomato wedges and olives.

***Note:** If seedless grapes are used, omit the lemon juice from ingredients.

CINNAMON BISCUITS

2 cans refrigerator buttermilk biscuits, cut in two
Melted butter *or* margarine
½ teaspoon ground cinnamon
¼ cup sugar

Take each piece of biscuit, dip in melted butter or margarine, then roll in the cinnamon and sugar mixture. Place on cookie sheet and bake according to manufacturer's directions.

RASPBERRY BISCUITS

1 can flaky refrigerator biscuits (10 to a can)
⅓ cup melted butter *or* margarine
¼ cup sugar
½ teaspoon ground cinnamon
Small jar raspberry preserves

Separate biscuits after removing from can and cut in half horizontally as one would slice a cake into layers. Take each half biscuit and dip in melted butter or margarine on both sides, then in sugar and cinnamon mixture. Place in lightly greased muffin cups or on a cookie sheet, placing ½ teaspoon preserves in the center of each. Bake for 10 to 12 minutes in 350° oven.

MACAROON TORTONI WITH STRAWBERRIES

¾ cup slivered toasted almonds
1 cup crumbled almond macaroons
1 cup heavy cream, whipped
3 tablespoons frozen orange juice concentrate, thawed
2 tablespoons orange-flavored liqueur (optional)
1 quart vanilla ice cream, slightly softened
2 to 3 cups strawberries, washed and hulled
2 to 3 tablespoons sugar

Sprinkle almonds and 2 tablespoons of macaroon crumbs in bottom of a 6½-cup mold (preferably one with a simple design). Whip cream until stiff and mix in orange concentrate, liqueur and remaining macaroons. Turn ice cream into a bowl and fold in whipped cream and macaroon mixture. Spoon into the mold, cover and freeze until firm (at least 4 hours or up to a week).

To serve, dip mold in a pan of warm water a few seconds and invert on a serving platter. Sprinkle strawberries with sugar to taste and spoon around ice cream mold.

Serves 8

SEAFOOD THERMIDOR • POINSETTIA SALAD
CRISP CRACKERS • STRAWBERRY CREPES

"An inexpensive but very tasty menu that's easy to prepare. It looks pretty, too."

STRAWBERRY CREPES

(See the basic crepe recipe included with French dinner menu on page 43 with the Crepes Frangipane.)

Strawberry filling:
2 pints fresh strawberries, washed, hulled and sliced
½ cup firmly packed light brown sugar
2 cups dairy sour cream *or* heavy cream, whipped
Confectioners' sugar
8 6-inch crepes

Toss sliced strawberries with brown sugar. Fill crepes with strawberries. Top with sour cream or sweetened whipped cream. Fold over. Sprinkle with confectioners' sugar. Garnish with more cream and strawberries. Serve at once.

SEAFOOD THERMIDOR

2 pounds sole *or* cod filets (fresh or frozen)
2 small onions, chopped
Lemon slice
½ cup water
2 10¾-ounce cans condensed cream of shrimp soup
6 tablespoons all-purpose flour
½ cup dry vermouth
½ cup milk
½ cup shredded mozzarella cheese
4 tablespoons chopped parsley
Salt to taste
2 cups soft bread crumbs
4 tablespoons grated Parmesan cheese
2 tablespoons butter *or* margarine
1 teaspoon paprika

Thaw frozen fish and skin, if necessary. Cut into ½-inch cubes. In saucepan, place onion, lemon slice and water; boil, covered, for 5 minutes. Add fish and simmer, covered, 5 to 6 minutes or until fish flakes easily.

In a small saucepan, blend soup and flour; gradually stir in dry vermouth and milk. Cook and stir until thickened and bubbly. Stir in mozzarella and parsley; heat through. Taste for salt.

Drain fish and onion; remove lemon slice. Fold fish into sauce. Spoon into 8 coquille shells or ramekin dishes. Combine bread crumbs, Parmesan cheese, butter or margarine and paprika. Sprinkle over fish and broil about 8 inches from heat until browned and bubbly.

POINSETTIA SALAD

8 medium, firm tomatoes, peeled
1 8-ounce package cream cheese, at room temperature
2 tablespoons dairy sour cream
1 tablespoon chopped chives (fresh or frozen)
2 tablespoons mayonnaise
3 drops Tabasco® pepper sauce
Paprika
Lettuce, washed, dried and chilled

Cut tomatoes in eighths, cutting about ⅔ way through without severing sections. Pull open to represent petals of flower. Chill. Beat cream cheese until smooth and fluffy. Add other ingredients except paprika and lettuce. Place a scoop of cream cheese in center of each tomato, dividing cheese mixture equally. Garnish with small amount of mayonnaise dusted with paprika. Place on whole lettuce leaf or shredded lettuce.

Serves 8

CHICKEN SALAD • HOT DEVILED CRAB
FRUIT MEDLEY WITH POPPY SEED DRESSING
RASPBERRY SHERBET • SESAME CRACKERS
ASSORTED MINTS AND COFFEE

"This attractive, easy-to-serve luncheon-on-a-plate lets you use your ingenuity in making an eye appealing arrangement. Two cold salads, dressed in greens, are placed to leave room for the hot deviled crab in a shell. The sherbet in a decorative dish is the accent note in the center of the plate. Don't spare parsley as a decorative touch."

FRUIT MEDLEY WITH POPPY SEED DRESSING

If possible, use fresh fruits, or a combination of frozen, fresh and canned. Bananas, oranges, pineapple and avocado are almost always available, as well as apples both red and golden-green. Make a colorful arrangement, leaving some pieces larger than others. If desired, a small scoop of cottage cheese would be a nice addition. Over this put the following dressing:

Poppy Seed Dressing:
½ cup mayonnaise
2 tablespoons sugar
1 tablespoon fresh lemon juice
1 tablespoon poppy seeds

Mix together well and pour over fruit just before serving.

CHICKEN SALAD

(See recipe for Chicken Salad with Garnish included with luncheon menu on page 23.)

HOT DEVILED CRAB

½ cup finely chopped onion
¼ cup finely chopped green pepper
3 tablespoons butter *or* margarine
3 tablespoons all-purpose flour
1½ cups half-and-half
2 egg yolks, slightly beaten
Dash of cayenne
½ teaspoon salt
2 teaspoons Worcestershire sauce
1 teaspoon prepared mustard
1 tablespoon finely chopped chives
2 7½-ounce cans crab meat, drained, flaked and cartilage removed
1 cup soft bread crumbs
3 tablespoons butter *or* margarine, melted

Heat oven to 375°. Sauté onion and green pepper in 3 tablespoons butter or margarine until tender. Add flour and mix until smooth. Stir in half-and-half gradually. Cook over medium heat, stirring constantly until sauce thickens. In small bowl, stir a small amount of the hot sauce into egg yolks. Add to remaining sauce in pan and heat for 2 or 3 minutes, stirring constantly. Remove from heat and add cayenne, salt, Worcestershire, mustard and chives. Mix well. Stir in crab meat.

Spoon crab mixture into 8 buttered ramekins, custard cups or shells. Combine bread crumbs and 3 tablespoons melted butter or margarine and sprinkle on crab mixture. Bake 20 to 25 minutes or until crumbs are golden brown and mixture is bubbly.

SHERBET

Choose a sherbet that will blend in with the food both in color and in taste. Raspberry would be an excellent selection. Crisp sesame crackers will be a good contrast in texture to serve as an accompaniment.

And, instead of dessert (which no one will have room for), pass an assortment of mints and serve little cups of hot coffee.

Serves 6

JELLIED CUCUMBER CONSOMMÉ
SALAD ASPARAGUS • SHRIMP DE JONGHE
SOUTHERN AMBROSIA

"Shrimp de Jonghe is very rich but so good. I have planned the rest of the menu to compensate for the richness of the shrimp dish."

SHRIMP DE JONGHE

1½ tablespoons real butter
½ tablespoon all-purpose flour
¾ cup half-and-half, scalded
¼ teaspoon salt
1½ pounds shrimp, cooked, shelled and deveined
Garlic salt
1½ cups coarsely crushed RITZ® crackers
1 cup real butter, melted
¼ cup finely chopped chives

Put 1½ tablespoons butter in saucepan and mix in the flour. Scald half-and-half and add, stirring constantly. Cook until thickened and add salt.

Put shrimp in buttered ramekin dishes, individual shells or in a shallow baking dish of your choice. Pour sauce over shrimp and sprinkle very lightly with garlic salt. Put cracker crumbs over shrimp mixture, then dribble melted butter over this. Sprinkle with chopped chives. Bake at 375° until hot and bubbly, about 10 to 12 minutes. Place under broiler to lightly brown top. Serve immediately.

SALAD ASPARAGUS

1½ pounds fresh asparagus, cleaned and trimmed *or* 2 10-ounce packages frozen asparagus
6 tablespoons olive oil *or* 3 tablespoons each olive oil and vegetable oil
1 teaspoon sugar
½ teaspoon dried basil
¼ teaspoon salt
⅛ teaspoon pepper
¼ cup fresh lemon juice

Cook asparagus until just tender; drain thoroughly. Beat other ingredients into thick sauce (use blender for smooth texture). Pour over hot asparagus and serve immediately.

JELLIED CUCUMBER CONSOMMÉ

3 10½-ounce cans beef consommé (gelatin added)
1 medium *or* 2 small cucumbers, peeled, seeded and minced
½ green pepper, minced
1 tablespoon minced chives *or* scallions (fresh or frozen)
Fresh parsley

Mix the ingredients well and ladle into soup cups or plates. Chill thoroughly, 3 or 4 hours, until set. Garnish with a tiny sprig of parsley before serving.

Note: Be sure to buy consommé which states "gelatin added" on the label.

SOUTHERN AMBROSIA

4 large oranges
1 13¼-ounce can pineapple tidbits
2 tablespoons orange-flavored liqueur *or* white rum *or* orange juice
4 medium bananas
4 tablespoons confectioners' sugar
1 1½-ounce can flaked coconut
6 maraschino cherries

Peel oranges, removing white membrane at same time. Cut oranges crosswise into ⅛-inch-thick slices. Drain pineapple, reserving syrup. Combine syrup and your choice of white rum, orange liqueur or orange juice and set aside. Peel bananas and cut diagonally into ⅛-inch-thick slices.

Combine all ingredients in a glass bowl, except the coconut flakes and cherries. Refrigerate until well chilled. Serve in individual dishes with coconut flakes and a cherry placed on each serving.

Dinner
Menus
Dick Dahlquist

Serves 6

SWEDISH PORK ROAST
CORN PUDDING • BUTTERED ASPARAGUS
STRAWBERRY-CRANBERRY SALAD
or
CRANBERRY-ROSÉ SALAD
FRUIT SALAD DRESSING • CREME CARAMEL

"Here's a different way of roasting pork. The Creme Caramel is a favorite gourmet dessert . . . and really so easy to do."

SWEDISH PORK ROAST

12 medium prunes, pitted
3 tablespoons butter *or* margarine
3 tablespoons vegetable oil
4½- to 5-pound pork loin, boned and tied
¾ cup dry vermouth
¾ cup heavy cream
Salt and freshly ground black pepper
¼ cup red currant jelly

Place prunes in saucepan, cover with water and bring to boil. Remove from heat and let soak in water 30 minutes. In casserole with lid, melt butter or margarine and vegetable oil over moderate heat until foam subsides. Add pork and brown on all sides. Remove all the fat from the casserole, pour in wine and heavy cream and bring to simmer while whisking. Add salt and pepper to taste. Cover pan and cook in center of oven for 1½ hours at 350° or until meat thermometer registers 170°. Add prunes the last 30 minutes of cooking, basting them well. Remove loin and prunes from pan and rest on heated platter, keeping warm.

Skim fat from liquid in pan and bring liquid to boil. When it has reduced to about 1 cup, stir in red currant jelly and simmer briefly until smooth. Serve meat garnished with prunes with the sauce served separately.

CORN PUDDING

1 1-pound can cream style corn
1 cup milk
1 egg, beaten
1 cup cracker crumbs
3 tablespoons canned pimiento, chopped
2 tablespoons chopped onion
2 tablespoons chopped green pepper
¾ teaspoon salt
Dash of pepper
½ cup cracker crumbs, buttered

Mix corn, milk and egg. Add 1 cup cracker crumbs, pimiento, onion, green pepper, salt and dash of pepper. Pour into greased 1½-quart baking dish. Top with buttered cracker crumbs and bake in 350° oven for 30 to 35 minutes, or until knife inserted off-center comes out clean.

STRAWBERRY-CRANBERRY SALAD

1 3-ounce package raspberry-flavored gelatin
1 cup boiling water
1 1-pound can whole cranberry sauce
1 10-ounce package frozen strawberries, thawed

Put raspberry-flavored gelatin in bowl, pour over boiling water and stir until dissolved. Let cool and place in refrigerator. Break cranberry sauce into bits. When gelatin begins to get thick, stir in the cranberry sauce and thawed strawberries. Pour into mold and set in refrigerator until firm.

CRANBERRY-ROSÉ SALAD

2 3-ounce packages raspberry-flavored gelatin
2 cups boiling water
1 1-pound can whole cranberry sauce
1 8¾-ounce can crushed pineapple, undrained
¾ cup rosé wine
½ cup coarsely chopped walnuts

Dissolve gelatin in boiling water. Stir in cranberry sauce, undrained pineapple and rosé wine. Chill until partially set. Fold in nuts. Pour mixture into a 6½-cup mold. Chill until firm.

FRUIT SALAD DRESSING

"Serve your choice of Strawberry-Cranberry Salad or Cranberry-Rosé Salad with mayonnaise or this delicious fruit salad dressing."

3 eggs, slightly beaten
½ cup sugar
Juice of 1 orange
Juice of 1 lemon
1 cup heavy cream, whipped

In top of double boiler, beat eggs and sugar together. Add juices, stirring well. Cook, stirring until thick. Cool and refrigerate. Just before serving, fold in 1 cup cream, whipped.

CREME CARAMEL

"An easy and quick dessert to make . . . delicious, too!"

Custard:

1 teaspoon vanilla
3 teaspoons powdered coffee +
2 tablespoons water (optional)
2 cups half-and-half, scalded
1 cup milk, scalded
3 whole eggs
3 egg yolks
½ cup sugar

Caramel:

1½ cups sugar
¼ cup water
Heavy cream, whipped

For custard, add vanilla and optional coffee dissolved in 2 tablespoons water to scalded half-and-half and milk. Let cool. Beat together 3 whole eggs and 3 yolks with ½ cup sugar. Gradually pour half-and-half mixture into egg mixture, stirring vigorously with a whisk.

For caramel, heat 1½ cups sugar in a heavy pan over very low heat. Stir constantly until sugar is melted and straw-colored. Remove pan from heat and add ¼ cup **very hot** water, ever so slowly. To make syrup heavier, return pan to low heat and continue stirring until sugar mixture is color of maple syrup. Pour into a 1-quart round oven dish (or in 6 individual custard cups), rotating the mold until the entire surface is well coated.

Let the caramel set, then pour in custard through a sieve. Set mold or custard cups in a pan of hot water. Bake in 350° oven for about 45 minutes, or until a knife inserted off-center comes out clean.

Cool custard and unmold onto a serving dish just before serving. To insure that the caramel comes out intact, loosen around the edge with tip of knife, then dip mold quickly into very hot water up to the rim as you would in releasing a gelatin. Rosettes of whipped cream may be used around base of mold for decoration.

BUTTERED ASPARAGUS

2½ pounds fresh asparagus *or*
2 packages frozen asparagus
¼ cup water
Butter *or* margarine
Salt and pepper to taste

For fresh asparagus, clean and stem. For either kind of asparagus, cut on bias into bite-size pieces and put in saucepan. (Cutting the asparagus spears on the bias assures you of tender asparagus.) Put ¼ cup water over the pieces and after bringing to boil, turn heat down to medium-low and cook until crisp-tender. Take care water does not evaporate completely. Add butter or margarine, salt and pepper to taste and shake to distribute evenly.

Russian Dinner Serves 6

KIEV BORSCHT • BEEF STROGANOFF
BUTTERED NOODLES • COSSACK SALAD
MAZURKA LEMON NUT CAKE

"It is always fun to impress your friends with foreign menus. This is a delicious one with a unique dessert."

KIEV BORSCHT

2 large beets, peeled and chopped *or* 2 cups canned beets
1 cup chopped red *or* green cabbage
2 medium onions, chopped
3 10½-ounce cans beef broth
Salt and pepper to taste
Dairy sour cream

Simmer vegetables in the broth until tender, about 30 to 40 minutes. Add salt and pepper to taste. Ladle into heavy pottery bowls and top with a tablespoon of sour cream on each serving.

COSSACK SALAD

½ cup cooked green beans, cut in pieces
½ cup diced cooked carrots
½ cup cooked green peas
1 small cucumber, cubed
6 radishes, coarsely chopped
6 scallions, trimmed and sliced
2 celery ribs, coarsely sliced
⅔ cup mayonnaise
1 teaspoon grated rind of lemon
1 tablespoon fresh lemon juice
Salt and pepper to taste
Lettuce, washed, dried and chilled

Toss all vegetables together. Mix mayonnaise, grated rind and juice of lemon and pour over vegetables. Sprinkle with salt and pepper to taste and let marinate at least a couple of hours before serving on a bed of lettuce leaves.

BEEF STROGANOFF

1½ pounds beef sirloin, cut in thin strips*
2 tablespoons all-purpose flour
½ teaspoon salt
3 tablespoons butter *or* margarine
3 tablespoons vegetable oil
½ pound fresh mushrooms, sliced
½ cup chopped onion
1 clove garlic, minced
3 tablespoons butter *or* margarine
3 tablespoons all-purpose flour
1 10½-ounce can beef broth
1 cup dairy sour cream
4 tablespoons dry vermouth *or* Burgundy

Coat strips of beef with mixture of 2 tablespoons flour and ½ teaspoon salt. Brown beef quickly in butter or margarine and vegetable oil and remove from skillet. Add mushrooms, onion and garlic; sauté for 4 minutes and remove. Add remaining 3 tablespoons butter or margarine; add 3 tablespoons flour and blend. Stir in broth and cook, stirring over medium heat until thickened. Return meat, mushrooms and onion mixture to skillet. (The beef may be held over until just before ready to serve. Heat slowly, then proceed with recipe.) Stir in sour cream and dry vermouth or Burgundy. Heat thoroughly (do not boil) and serve.

***For easy slicing,** place beef in freezer just until firm, but not frozen.

MAZURKA LEMON NUT CAKE

Cake filling:
6 egg yolks
¾ cup superfine sugar
Grated rind of 1 lemon (about 2 teaspoons)
2 tablespoons fresh lemon juice
8 ounces toasted, powdered almonds
6 egg whites
¼ teaspoon cream of tartar
4 tablespoons superfine sugar

Topping:
1 cup heavy cream, chilled
2 tablespoons rum (optional)
2 tablespoons confectioners' sugar

Preheat oven to 375°. Butter and sugar a 10-inch glass, ovenproof pie pan as you would oil and flour a pan for cake baking.

For cake filling, beat egg yolks for about 1 minute, then slowly pour in ¾ cup sugar, continuing to beat until mixture falls back upon itself in a ribbon when the beater is lifted. Beat in grated lemon rind and lemon juice to yolks. Fold in powdered nuts, reserving 1 tablespoon for decoration. (Powder almonds in food processor, nut grinder or blender.)

In another bowl, beat egg whites with cream of tartar until they form stiff peaks. Beat in 4 tablespoons of sugar, one at a time. Fold ⅓ of the egg whites into yolk mixture. Then put remaining yolk mixture over whites and continue to fold in carefully until all streaks of white disappear.

Pour batter into prepared pan and spread evenly to sides. Bake in center of oven for about 40 minutes, or until it has puffed and begins to draw slightly away from sides of pan. Turn off heat and let cake rest in oven for 15 minutes. Remove and turn out onto cake rack. When cold, transfer to cake plate.

For topping, beat cream until soft peaks form. Gradually beat in rum and confectioners' sugar until cream is stiff. Spread over cake and sprinkle top with reserved powdered nuts.

BUTTERED NOODLES

1 1-pound package egg noodles
1 tablespoon vegetable oil
2 tablespoons butter *or* margarine
1 tablespoon minced fresh parsley

Prepare noodles according to package directions adding 1 tablespoon vegetable oil to the boiling water. Drain the cooked noodles well, add butter or margarine, shaking pan so all noodles will be covered. Sprinkle with parsley just before serving.

Note: If noodles must be cooked ahead, after cooking and draining, add 1 tablespoon of vegetable oil. Just before serving, plunge noodles into boiling water for a few seconds to heat and loosen strands. After draining, add butter or margarine and parsley.

Serves 12

AVOCADO BOATS • CHICKEN ORIENTALE
SESAME-ORANGE SALAD
HOT BUTTERED FRENCH BREAD
CHOCOLATE CAKE • VANILLA ICE CREAM

"This is a great dinner for a crowd – so easy to put together. If you have too many for a sit-down dinner, I would suggest eliminating the avocado boats and serving them sometime at a ladies' luncheon."

AVOCADO BOATS

6 hard-cooked eggs, chopped
3 tablespoons finely chopped green onions
3 tomatoes, peeled, seeded and chopped
6 avocados, halved and pitted
6 tablespoons mayonnaise
1½ tablespoons fresh lemon juice
3 teaspoons prepared mustard
¾ teaspoon salt
Several drops Tabasco® pepper sauce
Lettuce, washed, dried and chilled
6 slices bacon, crisp-cooked, drained and crumbled

Combine eggs, onions and tomatoes. With melon-baller, carefully scoop out avocado halves leaving firm shells. To the avocado balls, add the remaining ingredients, except lettuce and bacon. Add egg mixture, folding carefully so as to keep avocado from breaking up. Spoon into avocado shells. Serve on lettuce bed. Sprinkle top of each boat with crumbled bacon.

CHICKEN ORIENTALE

"This is a great dinner for a crowd, so easy to put together."

- 6 cups chopped cooked chicken
- 2 10¾-ounce cans cream of mushroom soup
- 1 10¾-ounce can cream of chicken soup
- ½ pound fresh mushrooms, sliced and sautéed in 2 tablespoons butter or margarine *or* 1 6-ounce can sliced mushrooms
- 4 cups chopped celery
- 2 8½-ounce cans sliced water chestnuts
- 1 cup sliced almonds, lightly toasted
- 2 5-ounce (*or* 1 9½-ounce) cans Chinese noodles
- Paprika
- Soy sauce

Mix the first 6 ingredients together in a large bowl. Pour into a 12 x 16-inch baking dish which has been buttered. Bake 45 minutes in a 350° oven.

Leave in oven to keep warm while preparing the following: Place almonds and noodles in shallow pan with a lot of room. Toast about 10 to 12 minutes in 325° oven. Watch carefully, as they get too dark or burn easily. Put toasted noodle-nut combination on top of baked chicken and toss together just before serving. Add no salt, but sprinkle generously with paprika. Serve with soy sauce, if desired.

SESAME-ORANGE SALAD

- 2 heads lettuce, torn up
- 1 cup chopped green pepper
- 4 green onions, sliced
- 2 11-ounce cans mandarin orange sections, drained
- 1 medium cucumber, sliced

Dressing:

- 4 tablespoons sesame seeds
- 1 cup mayonnaise
- 1 cup French salad dressing
- 4 tablespoons grated Parmesan cheese
- 2 tablespoons sugar
- 2 tablespoons cider vinegar
- 1 teaspoon salt

In skillet, toast sesame seeds until lightly browned; set aside. Combine mayonnaise, French dressing, cheese, sugar, vinegar and salt; add sesame seeds. Combine lettuce, green pepper and onions. Arrange lettuce mixture, orange sections and cucumber in salad bowl. Pour salad dressing over this and toss lightly before serving.

Note: You may not need all of the dressing.

CHOCOLATE CAKE

⅓ cup butter *or* margarine
1 cup granulated sugar
1 egg
1½ cups unsifted all-purpose flour
⅓ cup cocoa
⅛ teaspoon salt
1 teaspoon baking soda
1 cup buttermilk
1 teaspoon vanilla

Frosting:
1½ cups confectioners' sugar
2 tablespoons cocoa
2 tablespoons butter *or* margarine, softened
3 tablespoons or more cold, strong coffee
½ teaspoon vanilla
⅛ teaspoon salt
Coarsely chopped walnuts

Cream ⅓ cup butter or margarine and sugar together; add egg and beat well. Measure flour and sift with cocoa and salt. Add soda to the buttermilk, then add alternately with the flour. Add vanilla. Pour into an oiled and floured 7 x 11-inch pan. Bake at 350° for 25 to 30 minutes.

Note: Do not adjust for high altitude.

For frosting, sift confectioners' sugar and cocoa together in a bowl; add 2 tablespoons butter or margarine, then coffee (enough to make a spreading consistency). Add vanilla and salt. Spread on cake and top with chopped walnuts.

Serves 8

CURRIED CHEESE SOUP
CORNISH HENS WITH ORANGE-GINGER SAUCE
BRAISED ONIONS AND MUSHROOMS
CROOK-NECK SQUASH PUDDING
STRAWBERRY MOUSSE

"I have always felt that Cornish Hens needed a pick up. The Orange-Ginger Sauce does just that.

CURRIED CHEESE SOUP

4 3-ounce packages cream cheese
2 cups canned beef consommé
¾ teaspoon curry powder
½ medium clove garlic, chopped
Salt to taste
Tiny Alaskan shrimp, canned, *or* tiny frozen shrimp
Chopped fresh parsley

Put in blender first 4 ingredients and blend at full speed until smooth. Add salt to taste. Refrigerate for several hours or overnight. Taste for salt.

To serve, fill chilled cups with soup and top with several of the tiny shrimp and a pinch of parsley for garnish.

Note: If desired, serve soup course before seating guests. If soup becomes too thick, add beef broth to thin.

CORNISH HENS WITH ORANGE-GINGER SAUCE

8 1-pound Cornish hens, thawed (if birds are slightly larger, use 4 and cut in half)*
Salt and pepper
½ cup butter *or* margarine, melted
½ cup water

Orange-Ginger Sauce:
½ cup shredded orange peel
3 tablespoons grated lemon peel
1½ cups orange juice
4 tablespoons fresh lemon juice
2 cups red currant jelly
1 cup Madeira wine (dry)
2 teaspoons dry mustard
1 teaspoon ground ginger (use 1 tablespoon grated fresh ginger, if obtainable)
½ teaspoon salt
Dash Tabasco® pepper sauce

Heat oven to 450°. Sprinkle cavity and outside of each hen with salt and pepper. Tie legs together and arrange breast side up in buttered, shallow roasting pan. Brush with butter or margarine. Roast uncovered for 15 minutes, then reduce oven heat to 375°. Turn birds breast side down and add ½ cup water and cover with foil loosely. Bake for 30 minutes. Turn breast side up and baste with drippings in pan. Continue basting from time to time and roast for another 15 minutes.

To make sauce, combine orange and lemon peels and orange and lemon juices in small saucepan. Bring to boil and cook over medium heat, uncovered, 15 minutes or until peel is tender. Add jelly, wine, mustard, ginger, salt and pepper sauce. Bring to boil, stirring; reduce heat and continue cooking at a simmer for another 10 to 15 minutes to reduce and thicken sauce. It should be like heavy cream.

To serve, arrange whole birds on platter and remove string from legs. Spoon sauce over them and serve. Any sauce remaining can be served separately.

***If 4 birds are used,** split and cook them cut side down in roaster. Baste the last 15 minutes of cooking period. The halves should not take more than 45 minutes total cooking time. Test to be sure.

CROOK-NECK SQUASH PUDDING

"Any type squash may be used, but it's especially good with crook-neck."

3 pounds small yellow crook-neck squash
½ cup chopped onion
½ cup butter *or* margarine, melted
3 eggs, well beaten
2 tablespoons sugar
1 teaspoon salt
½ teaspoon freshly ground black pepper
1½ cups coarsely crushed saltine crackers
3 tablespoons butter *or* margarine, melted

Wash, stem and cut the squash into fairly even slices. Boil or steam squash and chopped onion until barely tender. Drain thoroughly, then mash. Add butter or margarine and blend in well. Add well-beaten eggs with the seasonings. Butter baking dish and fill with squash mixture. Top with saltine crackers mixed with 3 tablespoons melted butter or margarine. Bake in 350 ° oven for 45 minutes or until set.

Note: This casserole may be put together ahead of time and baked just before serving.

BRAISED ONIONS AND MUSHROOMS

½ cup raw long-grain white rice
3 cups water
5 cups thinly sliced yellow onions
5 tablespoons butter *or* margarine
¾ pound fresh mushrooms, sliced
Salt and freshly grated black pepper
½ cup heavy cream
2 to 3 tablespoons milk
6 tablespoons grated Parmesan cheese
Finely minced fresh parsley

Boil rice for 5 minutes in water and drain. Sauté yellow onions in butter or margarine for about ½ hour slowly, turning often, so they do not brown. Add sliced mushrooms to onions and continue to sauté for 8 to 10 minutes. Add rice, salt and pepper and heavy cream. Cover and cook over low heat for 30 minutes, stirring from time to time. Do this much ahead and at serving time, add 2 to 3 tablespoons milk and grated cheese before reheating. Serve with sprinkling of finely minced parsley, if desired.

STRAWBERRY MOUSSE

"A light, airy mousse of luscious red berries; makes a fine ending to a great meal."

2 pints (4 cups) strawberries *or* 1 1-pound package frozen, unsugared strawberries, thawed
½ cup confectioners' sugar
1 envelope unflavored gelatin
½ cup cold water
⅓ cup granulated sugar
4 egg whites
¼ teaspoon cream of tartar
¼ cup confectioners' sugar
1 cup heavy cream, whipped

Prepare a collar for a 4-cup soufflé dish by measuring off wax paper long enough to encircle dish. Fold in half lengthwise (paper should be about 2 inches higher than rim of dish). Fasten collar with tape or string to make the rim.

Wash, hull and dry strawberries, if fresh. Reserve 6 of the finest for decoration. Purée berries 1 cup at a time in blender. Pour into bowl. Continue until all berries are puréed. Mix in ½ cup confectioners' sugar (taste for sweetness). In small saucepan, soften gelatin in ¼ cup water, add ⅓ cup granulated sugar and remaining ¼ cup water, and over low heat, stir continuously until gelatin and sugar dissolve. Cool. Stir cooled gelatin mixture into puréed strawberries. Put bowl in pan partially filled with ice and water to speed setting. Beat egg whites with cream of tartar added. When foamy, beat in ¼ cup confectioners' sugar, 2 tablespoons at a time, until stiff peaks form. Put aside 4 tablespoons of whipped cream for decoration. Fold meringue and remaining whipped cream into strawberry mixture until streaks disappear. Pour into prepared soufflé dish. Refrigerate 4 hours or until set.

Remove collar gently, freeing soufflé from wax paper, if necessary, with a small knife. Decorate with reserved whipped cream and halved strawberries.

French Dinner Serves 6

TOMATO QUICHE • CHICKEN IN ZINFANDEL WINE SAUCE
BUTTERED PARSLEY POTATOES
HENRI'S CAESAR SALAD • CREPES FRANGIPANE

"Zinfandel wine in this popular French chicken dish is better than any other wine I have ever used. The crepes are simply delicious. As a matter of fact, the whole menu is really good and easy to do."

CHICKEN IN ZINFANDEL WINE SAUCE

"A perfect recipe to make the day before as the flavors blend to perfection."

3 whole chicken breasts, skinned, halved and boned
6 chicken thighs, skinned
2½ teaspoons salt
½ teaspoon pepper
All-purpose flour
4 tablespoons butter *or* margarine
6 slices bacon, cut in 1" pieces
½ cup chopped onion
2 sprigs fresh parsley
1 bay leaf
½ teaspoon dried thyme
2 cups Zinfandel wine (California light red wine)
1 cup canned chicken broth or your own stock
12 small onions, peeled
3 tablespoons butter *or* margarine
¾ pound fresh mushrooms, cleaned and quartered
2 tablespoons cornstarch
¼ cup heavy cream
1 tablespoon butter *or* margarine
Fresh parsley

Dust chicken with salt, pepper and flour. Sauté in 4 tablespoons butter or margarine until golden brown; remove from skillet and keep warm. Add bacon to skillet and sauté a few minutes without browning; add ½ cup chopped onions, parsley, bay leaf, thyme, wine and chicken stock. Bring to boil and simmer 10 minutes without cover. Return chicken to skillet and cover. Simmer for ½ hour.

In a small skillet, simmer peeled onions in a small amount of water until tender-crisp, about 20 minutes. Remove onions from water (which should be almost evaporated) and sauté in 3 tablespoons butter or margarine until browned. Remove from pan; add quartered mushrooms and over high heat, brown, turning frequently. Add onions to mushrooms and heat for 1 or 2 minutes before adding to chicken on serving platter.

Remove chicken from sauce and keep warm. Discard bay leaf. Mix cornstarch with cream and add a bit of warm sauce to this mixture. Combine cream mixture with wine sauce and continue cooking and stirring until it thickens, about 5 minutes. Add 1 tablespoon butter or margarine to sauce in bits and quickly take off heat. Return chicken to sauce and simmer 1 or 2 minutes to heat through.

On heated platter, arrange chicken and surround with onions and mushrooms. Pour sauce overall and sprinkle with parsley.

Note: If made the day before, heat covered in a moderate oven.

TOMATO QUICHE

(See pastry recipe on page 22 with Crab Quiche for a 10-inch pie crust.)

2 tablespoons butter *or* margarine
1 medium onion, diced
3 large tomatoes, skinned, seeded and chopped
1 teaspoon salt
¼ teaspoon pepper
¼ teaspoon dried thyme, crushed
½ pound natural Swiss cheese, diced
3 eggs
Salt and pepper to taste
1 cup half-and-half *or* heavy cream for a richer filling
Fresh watercress or parsley

In saucepan, melt butter or margarine and sauté onion about 10 minutes. Add tomatoes, salt, pepper and thyme and continue cooking for 5 minutes, over high heat to reduce liquid. Put mixture into 10-inch pie crust (see recipe on page 22). Sprinkle the diced cheese over this. Beat eggs, add salt and pepper to taste and beat in cream. Pour over mixture in pie shell. Bake 10 minutes at 425°, then reduce heat to 375° and continue baking for about 35 minutes, or until pan contents are firm to the touch. Rest 10 minutes before cutting. Serve in wedges on plate garnished with watercress or parsley.

Note: Quiche may be made ahead and heated in a moderate oven just until warm.

BUTTERED PARSLEY POTATOES

6 medium russet potatoes
½ teaspoon salt
4 tablespoons butter *or* margarine
¼ cup heavy cream (optional)
Salt and pepper to taste
3 tablespoons finely chopped fresh parsley and chives mixed

Peel and cube potatoes. Barely cover with water, adding ½ teaspoon salt to the water. Boil until just tender, about 20 minutes. Drain and return pan to low heat, shaking to dry the potatoes. Add butter or margarine, optional cream, salt and pepper to taste and sprinkle with chopped herbs. Shake pan to distribute seasonings and herbs evenly over vegetables.

HENRI'S CAESAR SALAD

2 medium heads romaine lettuce
¼ cup grated Parmesan cheese
¼ cup grated Romano cheese
1 cup unseasoned croutons

Dressing:
¼ teaspoon dry mustard
¼ teaspoon freshly ground black pepper
½ teaspoon salt
Juice of ½ large lemon
6 filets of anchovies, washed in cold water and finely chopped
1 clove garlic, minced
1 egg, at room temperature
1¾ tablespoons Worcestershire sauce

Wash, dry and tear the lettuce into bite-size pieces and refrigerate. The two cheeses are to be mixed together and set aside. Do not mix salad together until ready to serve.

When ready to serve, mix all ingredients **for dressing** and blend with wire whisk, beating to incorporate the egg with other ingredients.

Mix romaine, croutons and cheeses. Pour dressing over greens, tossing so each leaf is coated. Serve immediately in chilled bowls.

Note: This salad can be tossed and served at the table.

CREPES FRANGIPANE

"The crepes and almond cream can be made ahead and assembled before serving."

Basic crepes:
1¼ cups all-purpose flour
½ teaspoon granulated sugar
⅛ teaspoon salt
3 eggs
1½ cups milk
2 tablespoons butter *or* margarine, melted and cooled
Butter or margarine for cooking, melted

Filling for Crepes Frangipane:
¾ cup milk
2 tablespoons granulated sugar
2½ tablespoons all-purpose flour
2 egg yolks
½ teaspoon vanilla
¼ teaspoon almond extract
1 tablespoon butter *or* margarine
1½ teaspoons grated orange rind
2 to 3 macaroons, crushed
1½ teaspoons brandy
Confectioners' sugar

For basic crepes, mix all ingredients except butter or margarine for cooking in blender, or mix by hand, beating well. Refrigerate several hours or overnight. Mix well before using and add a couple tablespoons of milk if too thick (the batter should be the consistency of thick cream). **To cook crepes,** use a regular French, iron crepe pan if you have one; if not, a Teflon-lined frying pan works very well. The pan should be 8 to 9 inches in diameter with sides sloping to a bottom of 6 inches in diameter. Place pan on medium-high heat; let the pan get good and hot, then brush with melted butter or margarine. The butter should sizzle but not brown or burn. The secret of a tender crepe is to use just enough batter to cover the bottom of the pan in a thin layer. Dip your ladle into the batter and scoop up about 3 tablespoons. Pour the batter into the pan with your left hand and holding the handle of the pan with your right hand, raise the pan from the heat and tilt it so the batter quickly swirls around and runs over the bottom of the pan. Replace the pan on the heat and bake the crepe until lightly browned. An easy way to turn crepes is to use a rubber spatula. Run the spatula around the edges of the crepes then slide the spatula underneath and with a quick movement, flip it over using your hand if needed. Makes 16 to 20 6-inch crepes.

For filling, heat milk to boiling. In another saucepan, mix sugar, flour and egg yolks. Slowly pour in hot milk, whisking mixture continuously over medium heat. Cook until it coats the back of a spoon rather heavily. Remove from heat and add vanilla, almond extract, butter or margarine, grated orange rind and macaroons. Stir in brandy. To keep film from forming on sauce, cover with a piece of wax paper and top the pan with a lid. Makes 16 to 20 6-inch crepes.

To assemble, take crepes 1 at a time and put 1 tablespoon of almond cream in center of each. Fold in half and then in quarters. Place in a shallow buttered serving dish in 200° oven to keep slightly warm. Sprinkle with confectioners' sugar and serve 2 to each person.

Mexican Dinner Serves 6

GAZPACHO • CHICKEN ENCHILADAS
MEXICAN RICE • PASTEL DE ELOTE—CORN PIE
GUACAMOLE-PINEAPPLE SALAD
CAPIROTADA—BREAD PUDDING

"Most everyone likes Mexican food if it isn't too hot. These recipes are just right for our tastes. If you have guests who prefer a hotter dish, give them a jar of hot crushed red pepper to add to their food."

CHICKEN ENCHILADAS

3 whole chicken breasts and 3 thighs or 1 3½- to 4-pound chicken
1 teaspoon salt
Celery tops
1 onion studded with 3 cloves
2 onions, chopped
3 tablespoons vegetable oil
1 clove garlic, minced
Salt and pepper to taste
1 3½-ounce can green chilies, chopped and seeded (4 chilies)
1 tablespoon sugar
4 cups canned enchilada sauce (mild or medium)
12 corn tortillas
¼ cup vegetable oil
2½ cups half-and-half
6 chicken bouillon cubes
¾ pound grated Monterey Jack cheese

Simmer chicken until tender in water to which salt, celery tops and clove studded onion have been added. Cool chicken in stock. Remove chicken, skin and bone and cut into bite-size pieces. Sauté chopped onions in 3 tablespoons vegetable oil until soft. Add garlic, salt and pepper to taste, green chilies, sugar, enchilada sauce and simmer 10 minutes. Add chicken and simmer for 5 minutes.

Heat the corn tortillas in ¼ cup vegetable oil until pliable (this takes only a few seconds for each). Remove excess oil on paper towel, then fill each tortilla with about ⅓ cup of chicken mixture. Roll and place in a shallow greased casserole in a single layer with seam side down. (Recipe may be completed to this point and refrigerated or even frozen.) Heat half-and-half and bouillon cubes in a saucepan, being sure cubes are dissolved. Pour this mixture over enchiladas and sprinkle with grated cheese. Bake at 350° for 30 to 40 minutes until hot and bubbly.

PASTEL DE ELOTE—CORN PIE

"This is a hearty cornbread, almost a vegetable."

- 1 cup yellow corn meal
- ½ teaspoon baking soda
- ¾ teaspoon salt
- 1 small onion, finely chopped
- 1 clove garlic, chopped
- 1 cup canned cream style corn
- 3 eggs
- ¼ cup bacon drippings *or* vegetable oil
- 1 cup dairy sour cream
- 2 canned green chilies, seeded and minced
- 1 cup grated Cheddar cheese

Mix corn meal, soda, salt, onion, garlic, corn, eggs, bacon drippings or oil, sour cream and chili peppers. Beat well. Spread ½ of the mixture in buttered 10-inch iron skillet or a 10-inch round baking pan. Sprinkle the cheese over the batter. Cover with remaining batter. Bake for 45 minutes at 350° until browned. Serve hot with butter.

Note: This may be made ahead of time and reheated, wrapped in foil. It also takes well to freezing.

GUACAMOLE-PINEAPPLE SALAD

- 3 ripe avocados
- 3 tablespoons fresh lemon *or* lime juice, *or* to taste
- ½ teaspoon salt *or* to taste
- ½ teaspoon ground coriander seed
- 2 canned green chilies, rinsed, seeded and chopped
- 1 medium tomato, finely chopped
- Tabasco® pepper sauce to taste (optional)
- Canned sliced pineapple
- Lettuce, washed, dried, chilled
- Paprika

Cut avocados in half, remove seeds and scoop out pulp with a spoon or if skin is thin, peel the avocados. Mash pulp coarsely with a fork while blending in lemon or lime juice. Add salt and coriander. Add chopped chilies, tomato and optional pepper sauce. Place a round of sliced pineapple on a couple of lettuce leaves for each serving. Top with about ⅓ cup of the avocado mixture. Sprinkle with a bit of paprika.

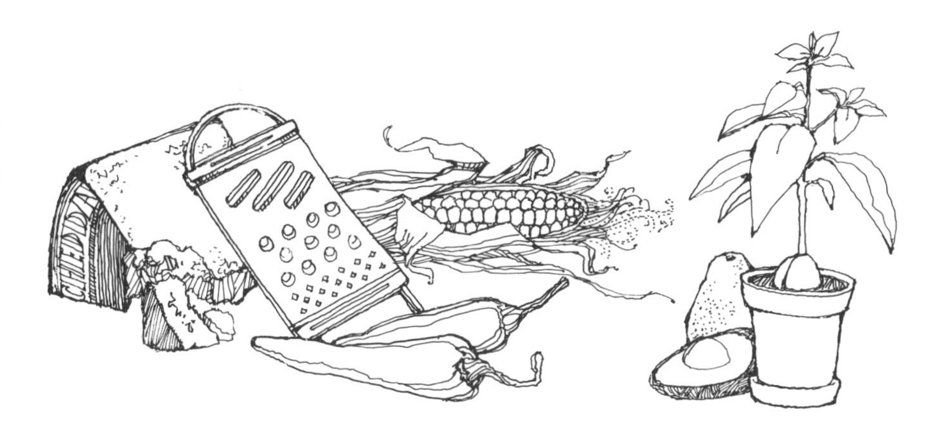

GAZPACHO

- 1 large cucumber, peeled and seeded
- 1 small green pepper, seeded
- ½ medium onion, coarsely chopped
- 4½ cups tomato juice
- 2 large tomatoes, peeled and seeded
- ⅓ cup olive oil
- ⅓ cup red wine vinegar
- ¼ teaspoon Tabasco® pepper sauce
- 1½ teaspoons salt
- ⅛ teaspoon pepper
- ¼ teaspoon garlic powder
- Finely chopped fresh parsley
- Croutons

In blender, put cucumber, green pepper, onion and 2 cups tomato juice and blend in spurts (turning machine on and off to control degree of fineness of ingredients) until vegetables are medium-coarsely ground. Remove to large bowl. In blender, put prepared tomatoes and 2 cups tomato juice and in spurts blend until tomatoes are medium-coarse. Remove and add to the large bowl. Add the remaining ½ cup tomato juice to blender with olive oil, wine vinegar, pepper sauce, salt, pepper and garlic powder. Blend. Remove and add to other ingredients. Mix contents of bowl until well blended and chill. Serve with a sprinkling of finely chopped parsley and croutons if desired.

Note: Gazpacho flavor improves with time, so it is better to make it a day or two before serving.

MEXICAN RICE

- 3 tablespoons bacon fat
- ⅔ cup chopped onion
- 1 cup raw long-grain white rice
- 1 cup chopped green pepper
- ½ cup chopped red bell pepper *or* ¼ cup pimiento, chopped
- 1 teaspoon chili powder
- 1½ teaspoons salt
- 2¼ cups water
- ½ of 10-ounce package frozen peas
- ½ of 10-ounce package frozen yellow corn
- 1 tablespoon butter *or* margarine
- Freshly ground black pepper

Melt bacon fat in heavy skillet. Sauté onions and rice until rice is opaque, but not browned. Add green and red bell peppers or pimiento, chili powder and 1 teaspoon salt. Mix well and add 2 cups water and bring to boil uncovered; reduce heat to very low and cover. Cook for about 18 to 20 minutes, or until tender.

To corn and peas, add ¼ cup water in saucepan and ½ teaspoon salt. Bring to boil and simmer 2 minutes. Turn up heat and reduce water from vegetables. Add butter or margarine and grind of pepper. Carefully fold peas and corn mixture into rice and keep hot, until serving.

Note: This dish may be made ahead of time and refrigerated until 1 hour before serving. Put into 350° oven for about 20 minutes or until very hot.

CAPIROTADA—BREAD PUDDING

"This is the best of many variations of this dessert and you'll think so, too."

¾ cup firmly packed brown sugar
½ teaspoon ground cinnamon
¼ teaspoon ground cloves
¾ cup water
3½ cups French bread crumbs (cut in ½-inch squares, crust and all)
1 cup raisins *or* a combination of raisins and currants
1 cup chopped walnuts
¾ cup sharp Cheddar cheese, finely diced
2 teaspoons butter *or* margarine
Vanilla ice cream *or* heavy cream, whipped and sweetened with 2 tablespoons confectioners' sugar

In saucepan, combine brown sugar, cinnamon, cloves and water, and boil gently until sugar is dissolved. Pour the hot syrup over bread cubes and toss gently. Add raisins (or mixture of raisins and currants), walnuts and cheese and toss again until blended. Butter a 1½-quart casserole or baking pan, and spoon mixture in evenly. This will be quite thick. Bake in 375° oven for about 15 to 20 minutes or until thoroughly heated through. Serve either warm or cold with ice cream or sweetened whipped cream.

Serves 8

JULIENNE VEGETABLE SOUP
TURKEY BREAST MADEIRA • BARLEY CASSEROLE
MARINATED SLICED TOMATOES
ITALIAN GARLIC LOAF • RASPBERRY CREAM

"One of the easiest menus in the book but so good. It's quite simple to increase for a larger group, too."

RASPBERRY CREAM

1 3-ounce package raspberry-flavored gelatin
½ cup boiling water
1 pint vanilla ice cream, softened
1 10-ounce package frozen raspberries, thawed
Heavy cream, whipped

Dissolve gelatin in boiling water. Add ice cream, stir until dissolved, then add raspberries. Refrigerate until set, at least 2 hours. Spoon into serving glasses and return to refrigerator until ready to serve. A dollop of whipped cream may be centered on each serving.

JULIENNE* VEGETABLE SOUP

"The addition of the julienne cut vegetables to the broth enriches the flavor."

16 cups canned beef broth
2 carrots, cut in julienne strips
1 medium potato, cut in julienne strips
1 small turnip, cut in julienne strips
1 small onion, cut in julienne strips
½ teaspoon dried marjoram, crushed
Salt and pepper to taste
Croutons

In a saucepan, bring the broth, carrots, potato, turnip, onion and marjoram to a boil. Salt and pepper to taste. Cover and reduce heat; simmer 15 to 20 minutes or until vegetables are tender. Serve hot with croutons made from dried bread slices, which have been buttered, diced and dried out in a slow oven.

***Julienne** means to cut food into long thin strips, resembling matchsticks.

MARINATED SLICED TOMATOES

6 large tomatoes
⅓ cup vegetable oil
1 tablespoon + 1 teaspoon fresh lemon juice
½ teaspoon minced garlic
½ teaspoon salt
½ teaspoon dried oregano leaves, finely rubbed
2 tablespoons minced fresh parsley

Peel and slice tomatoes in fairly thick slices. Combine and beat together vegetable oil, lemon juice, garlic, salt and oregano. Pour over tomatoes. Refrigerate covered for several hours until well chilled. Sprinkle with parsley just before serving.

BARLEY CASSEROLE

4 tablespoons butter *or* margarine
1 large onion, finely chopped
½ pound fresh mushrooms, cleaned (caps sliced, stems chopped)
1 cup pearl barley
Salt and pepper to taste
3 cups canned chicken *or* beef broth, boiling
¼ cup slivered toasted almonds

Heat butter or margarine in skillet and sauté onion 4 minutes. Add mushrooms and sauté another 4 minutes, stirring occasionally. Add barley and salt and pepper to taste to vegetables and brown lightly, mixing well. Add enough boiling broth to cover barley mixture by ½ inch. Pour into casserole, cover and bake in 350° oven for 25 minutes. Taste for doneness; if not done, add more boiling broth and continue cooking until barley is tender and liquid is absorbed. Before serving, sprinkle slivered almonds over barley.

ITALIAN GARLIC LOAF

Rub a peeled garlic clove over crusty Italian loaf. Crust acts as a grater. Slice loaf, butter and wrap in foil. Heat in oven before serving.

TURKEY BREAST MADEIRA

6 tablespoons butter *or* margarine
8 slices cooked turkey breast, ¼-inch thick
8 thin slices prosciutto *or* boiled ham
16 fresh mushrooms, washed, stemmed and left whole
Salt and pepper to taste
8 slices mozzarella cheese (1 8-ounce package)
½ cup heavy cream
½ cup Madeira wine (dry)
2 tablespoons chopped fresh parsley

In a large skillet, heat 4 tablespoons butter or margarine and sauté turkey slices to coat well. Remove and keep warm. Add a bit more butter or margarine if needed, and sauté ham slices for about 1 minute on each side. Remove and keep warm. Sauté mushroom caps in the same skillet for 5 minutes; sprinkle with salt and pepper.

In an attractive, shallow oven platter, arrange the turkey slices overlapping. Then alternate 1 slice each of ham and mozzarella cheese on the turkey slices. Place the mushroom caps around the meat-cheese combination. Mix the cream and Madeira together, pour over the meat mixture, spooning over mushrooms. Add sprinkle of pepper. Bake in 350° oven 15 to 20 minutes, basting a couple of times, just long enough to heat through and melt cheese. Sprinkle with parsley just before serving.

Note: For the busy hostess, the sliced meats can be purchased at the delicatessen. All can be assembled ahead and heated through at the last minute.

Serves 6

STANDING RIB ROAST
or
RUMP ROAST or CHUCK ROAST IN FOIL
GREEN BEANS or ASPARAGUS IN SEASON • HERB BREAD
GREEN CHILI RICE or CASSEROLE POTATOES
PERFECTION SALAD • MERINGUE NUT PIE

"Here are some good recipes to accompany our good old American favorite – beef."

STANDING RIB ROAST

5- to 6-pound standing rib roast
Salt and pepper
1 clove garlic (optional)

At least 3 to 4 hours before serving, place room temperature roast in a shallow pan, fat side up resting on bones on a rack, and sprinkle with salt and pepper. Rub with garlic clove split in half (optional). Place in preheated 375° oven **for exactly 45 minutes.** Do not add water. Do not cover. Do not baste. Turn off oven. Leave the roast in the oven, with the door closed. Do not open the oven. Turn oven on again at 375° for another 45 minutes before serving. Remove from oven. Let stand 15 minutes before carving.

Note: For roasts 10 to 12 pounds, leave in oven 60 minutes at the beginning and 60 to 90 minutes at the end for medium rare.

"Either one of the two following roasts is delicious and perfect for a family meal or for company."

RUMP ROAST

Select a 4- to 5-pound rump roast. Wipe and season with salt and pepper. Slice a medium onion over the top of the roast. Put in heavy Dutch oven-type pot and roast in 325° oven for approximately 4 hours.

CHUCK ROAST IN FOIL

Select a pot roast weighing about 4 or 5 pounds. Place a package of dry onion soup on heavy duty foil large enough to cover the roast. Put roast on top of this mixture. Spread 1 can mushroom soup over the meat. Bring the edges of the foil together and seal completely. Bake at 350° for approximately 4 hours or until tender.

GREEN CHILI RICE

"Do not combine this recipe until ready to bake."

1 cup raw long-grain white rice, cooked
2 cups dairy sour cream
Salt to taste
1 6-ounce can peeled green chilies, seeded and chopped
½ pound Monterey Jack cheese, cubed
½ cup grated Parmesan cheese

To the hot cooked rice, add sour cream and salt to taste. Add green chilies and Monterey Jack cheese, mixing well. Turn into 1½-quart buttered casserole and sprinkle with Parmesan cheese. Heat in 350° oven for 30 minutes. Serve from the casserole.

CASSEROLE POTATOES

8 to 10 medium russet potatoes
1 8-ounce package cream cheese, softened
⅔ cup dairy sour cream
½ cup minced green onions
8 slices crisp fried bacon, finely diced
Salt and pepper to taste
2 tablespoons butter *or* margarine, melted
2 tablespoons finely minced fresh parsley

Peel and boil potatoes in salted water until tender. Drain and return pan to low heat, shaking to dry the potatoes. Cream together cream cheese and sour cream with electric mixer. Add hot potatoes 1 at a time to the cream mixture and continue beating. Add green onions, diced bacon, salt and pepper to taste. Put in well-buttered ovenproof casserole. Drizzle 2 tablespoons melted butter or margarine over the top. Bake in 375° oven for 20 to 25 minutes, or until hot through. Remove and sprinkle with finely minced parsley before serving.

Note: This is perfect to prepare ahead and bake at the last minute.

PERFECTION SALAD

"This can be made in a ring mold and for a colorful addition, fill the center with sliced cooked carrots marinated in Italian dressing."

2 tablespoons unflavored gelatin
1½ cups cold water
1½ cups boiling water
½ cup sugar
1 teaspoon salt
½ cup cider vinegar
2 tablespoons fresh lemon juice
2 cups finely shredded cabbage
1 cup chopped celery
½ cup chopped green pepper
¼ cup diced, canned pimiento
⅓ cup sliced stuffed green olives
Carrot curls
Ripe olives
Mayonnaise

In a mixing bowl, combine gelatin and ½ cup cold water. Let soften, add boiling water and stir until gelatin dissolves. Add sugar and salt and stir until dissolved. Add remaining 1 cup cold water, vinegar and lemon juice. Chill until mixture is partially set. Add cabbage, celery, green pepper, pimiento and slices of stuffed green olives. Pour into a 6½-cup ring mold. Chill until firm. Unmold on round platter and fill center with marinated carrots, if desired. Garnish with carrot curls and ripe olives and serve with mayonnaise.

HERB BREAD

"Do this ahead; it's delicious."

- 1 loaf French bread
- 1 cup butter *or* margarine, softened
- 2 tablespoons finely chopped green onion
- 2 tablespoons finely chopped ripe olives
- 2 tablespoons finely chopped fresh parsley
- 1 teaspoon dried basil, crushed
- ½ teaspoon dried thyme, crushed
- ½ teaspoon dried marjoram, crushed
- ½ teaspoon dried tarragon, crushed

Slice French bread diagonally almost through to bottom crust. Blend softened butter or margarine with remaining ingredients; combine well. Spread cut surfaces of slices with mixture. Wrap loaf in heavy foil. Place on baking sheet and heat at 350° for 15 to 20 minutes. Serve hot.

MERINGUE NUT PIE

- 3 egg whites, at room temperature
- ⅛ teaspoon cream of tartar
- 1 cup granulated sugar
- 1 teaspoon vanilla
- 20 RITZ® crackers, crushed
- 1 teaspoon baking powder
- 1 cup chopped pecans *or* walnuts
- 1 cup heavy cream, whipped *or* vanilla ice cream
- 2 tablespoons confectioners' sugar
- Grated semi-sweet chocolate

Beat egg whites until foamy, then add cream of tartar and continue beating. After they begin to hold shape, add sugar 2 tablespoons at a time, beating until stiff peaks form. Add vanilla and beat into meringue. Remove beaters. Fold in crackers, baking powder and nuts. Spoon batter into a 10-inch buttered, glass oven dish. Bake in 350° oven on middle rack for 25 minutes. Turn off heat and let remain in oven another 15 minutes. Cool completely on rack, then spread with whipped cream to which 2 tablespoons confectioners' sugar has been added. A few gratings of semi-sweet chocolate on top are a nice touch.

Note: If desired, serve with ice cream instead of whipped cream.

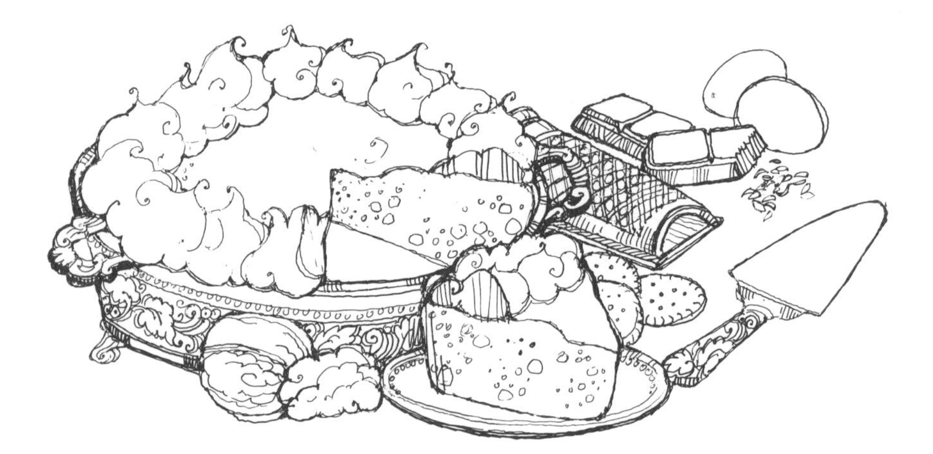

Chinese Dinner Serves 6

EGG DROP SOUP or EGG FLOWER TOMATO SOUP
BEEF AND VEGETABLES • FRIED RICE
JELLIED DIAMONDS WITH MANDARIN ORANGES
ALMOND COOKIES

"You don't need a wok to prepare a good Chinese dinner. To make preparation easier, chop, slice and assemble ingredients ahead of time. Two frying pans help to simplify the last minute cooking."

EGG DROP SOUP

2 13¾-ounce cans chicken broth *or* 2 cups boiling water into which 4 chicken bouillon cubes have been dissolved
½ cup diced water chestnuts
1 tablespoon cornstarch
2½ tablespoons cold water
¼ cup green onion, cut in ¼-inch pieces
1 egg, slightly beaten

Bring chicken broth to boiling in large saucepan. Add water chestnuts and cook for another ½ minute. Dissolve cornstarch in cold water. Add some hot soup to cornstarch mix; stir cornstarch into soup in saucepan. Stir until soup thickens. Add onion. Remove from heat and slowly pour in egg while stirring gently.

FRIED RICE

½ pound bacon, cut in ¼-inch pieces
3 eggs, beaten
1 tablespoon water
4 tablespoons vegetable oil
1⅓ cups raw long-grain white rice, cooked
4 tablespoons soy sauce
½ teaspoon salt
½ cup green onions, cut in ¼-inch pieces

Cut bacon into pieces, then fry, drain and keep warm. Beat eggs until whites and yolks are well mixed, adding 1 tablespoon water while beating. Using 1 tablespoon vegetable oil in skillet, add beaten eggs and slowly fry in large pancake size, leaving flat. Remove to plate and when cooled, slice into strips, ½ by 4 inches. Set aside.

Heat 3 tablespoons vegetable oil in clean skillet or wok and add the cold rice. Over high heat, coat rice with oil before blending in soy sauce and salt. Add green onions, egg strips, bacon and mix thoroughly.

Note: All components of this recipe can be prepared ahead, heated and assembled before serving.

BEEF AND VEGETABLES

1½ pounds sirloin of beef, sliced ¼-inch thick, 2 inches long
¼ cup soy sauce
2 tablespoons fresh lemon juice
¼ cup dry sherry
½ teaspoon onion powder
½ teaspoon garlic powder
3 tablespoons firmly packed brown sugar
Dash of pepper
4 tablespoons peanut oil for frying
2 medium green bell peppers, sliced *or* 1 each red and green bell pepper
1 zucchini squash, quartered and sliced
1 yellow crook-neck squash, quartered and sliced
2 celery ribs, thinly sliced
½ pound fresh mushrooms, sliced
1 tablespoon cornstarch
¼ cup beef stock
6 scallions, trimmed and cut in 1-inch slices

Prepare beef and marinate in soy sauce mixed with lemon juice, sherry, onion and garlic powders, brown sugar and a dash of pepper. Beef should marinate about 2 hours, turning frequently. Drain and reserve marinade. In wok or large skillet, heat almost to smoking 3 tablespoons peanut oil and cook meat, tossing for 2 or 3 minutes. Remove, place in bowl. Add 1 tablespoon peanut oil to wok, if needed, and add peppers. Sauté for 1 or 2 minutes. Remove and place with meat. Add zucchini and yellow squash to pan and cook for 2 to 3 minutes, tossing; remove. Add celery and mushrooms and toss for 2 or 3 minutes; remove. Mix cornstarch with beef broth, then add the reserved marinade. Put into wok or skillet and while stirring, cook until mixture thickens. Return all other cooked ingredients and toss in sauce for 1 or 2 minutes. Add scallions and give final toss.

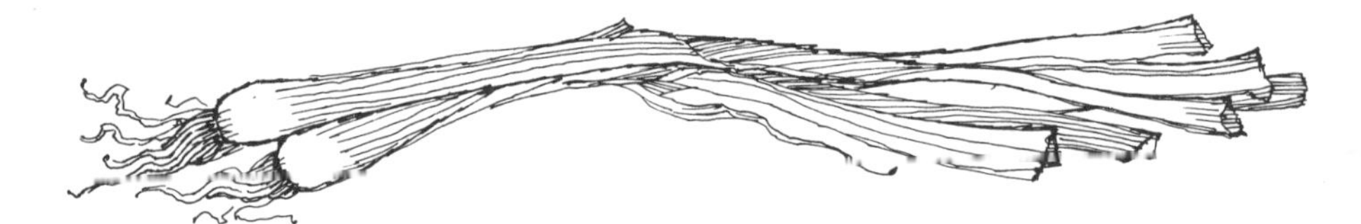

ALMOND COOKIES

½ cup sugar
½ cup butter *or* margarine
1 egg
1 teaspoon almond extract
Yellow food coloring
¼ cup ground almonds
1½ cups all-purpose flour
1 teaspoon baking powder

Glaze:
1 egg yolk
1 tablespoon water
¼ cup whole almonds, blanched

In bowl mix sugar, butter or margarine and whole egg, beating until fluffy. Add extract and yellow food coloring (about 2 or 3 drops). Beat in ¼ cup ground almonds (grind almonds in food processor, nut grinder or blender), flour and baking powder. Mix well. Dough will be stiff. Take a spoonful of dough and roll into ball. Place on greased cookie sheet. Continue until all dough is used. With spatula or fork, flatten dough into round.

For glaze, mix well, 1 egg yolk with 1 tablespoon water. Brush dough with egg glaze and press ½ almond in middle of each cookie. Bake at 350° for about 20 minutes until just turning brown. Remove from sheet and cool on rack.

EGG FLOWER TOMATO SOUP

1 onion, thinly sliced
4 tomatoes, skinned, seeded and chopped
1 tablespoon vegetable oil
4 cups canned chicken broth
Salt and pepper to taste
1 egg, beaten
Fresh parsley

Sauté onion and tomatoes in vegetable oil for 5 minutes without browning. Pour off oil, add broth and seasonings and simmer for 30 minutes. Add beaten egg, pouring slowly while stirring constantly until egg separates into shreds. Serve with a tiny piece of parsley floating on top.

JELLIED DIAMONDS WITH MANDARIN ORANGES

Jellied Diamonds:
1 tablespoon unflavored gelatin
6 tablespoons sugar
2 cups half-and-half
1 teaspoon almond extract

Sauce:
4 tablespoons sugar
1 tablespoon cornstarch
2 cups orange juice
1 tablespoon fresh lemon juice
1 tablespoon orange-flavored liqueur (optional)
1 11-ounce can mandarin oranges, drained

For Jellied Diamonds, combine gelatin and sugar in saucepan. Stir in 1 cup half-and-half and over low heat, stir constantly until sugar and gelatin dissolve. Do not boil. Let cool, then stir in almond extract and the remaining cup of half-and-half. Pour into a 9-inch square pan and refrigerate until set.

For sauce, mix sugar and cornstarch; add orange juice and blend. Over medium heat, stir until thickened. Remove from heat, add lemon juice and orange-flavored liqueur. Refrigerate until cold. Stir in mandarin oranges, keeping cold until ready to serve.

To serve, cut the gelatin into bite-size diamond shapes and place in glass serving bowl. Add the sauce and carefully mix so gelatin diamonds appear to float. Be sure to scoop up some of the orange sections when serving. Serve with Almond Cookies (see recipe on page 54).

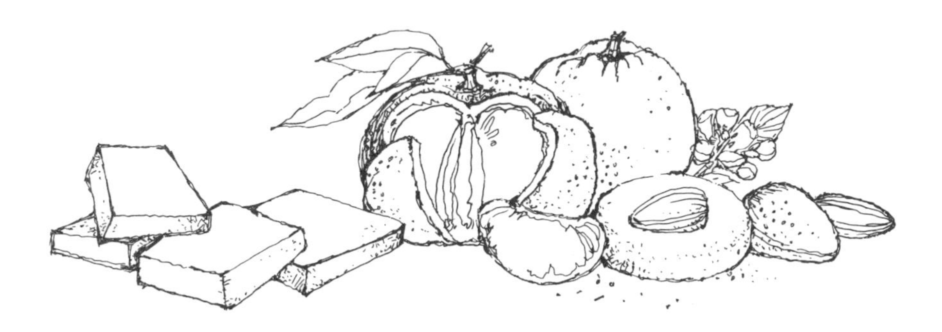

Serves 6

BEEF BURGUNDY WITH CROUTONS
MARJORAM BOILED POTATOES
BUTTERED PEAS AND ONIONS
LETTUCE GREENS WITH ROQUEFORT DRESSING
CHOCOLATE ROYALE

"Beef Burgundy – one of the most famous French dishes – is flavorful and economical. Make it in the morning so that the flavors can blend. You can make the Chocolate Royale days ahead. This is an easy but delicious menu that will delight your guests."

BEEF BURGUNDY WITH CROUTONS

1 pound salt pork
2 pounds chuck roast, fat removed
All-purpose flour
Salt and pepper
2 onions, thick sliced
2 cloves garlic, diced
4 beef bouillon cubes
1½ cups hot water
1 cup California Burgundy
½ pound fresh mushrooms, sliced
4 to 6 hard rolls
Butter *or* margarine, softened
½ cup finely minced fresh parsley

Cube pork, place in a saucepan and add water to barely cover; bring to boil and simmer for 10 minutes. (This removes excess salt.) Drain. Brown slowly in skillet in its own fat; remove to Dutch oven. Cube beef, removing gristly parts; dredge in flour, salt and pepper. Brown in some fat from salt pork using high heat. Remove meat from skillet and put in Dutch oven with pork, onions, garlic, bouillon cubes dissolved in hot water and Burgundy. Cook covered on top of stove over low heat for 2 hours or in oven for 2 hours at 350°, until meat is fork tender. Add sliced mushrooms and cook ½ hour longer. Taste for salt and pepper.

For garnish dry buttered, thinly sliced hard rolls in oven on cookie sheet at 350°. Watch closely so that they do not get too brown. Dip one end of the slice into meat juice, then into very finely minced parsley. Put beef on platter and surround with parsley garnished bread slices.

BUTTERED PEAS AND ONIONS

2 10-ounce packages frozen peas with pearl onions
Butter *or* margarine
Salt and pepper to taste

Cook according to directions on package and toss with butter or margarine, salt and pepper to taste.

MARJORAM BOILED POTATOES

12 small new potatoes, *or* russet potatoes, peeled and quartered
4 tablespoons butter *or* margarine
Salt and freshly ground black pepper
1 teaspoon dried marjoram, finely crushed

Boil potatoes until tender. Drain and return pan to low heat, shaking to dry the potatoes. Add butter or margarine, salt and freshly ground black pepper and toss with the crushed marjoram until well coated.

LETTUCE GREENS WITH ROQUEFORT DRESSING

1 head romaine lettuce *or* mixed salad greens
4 scallions, minced
1 tablespoon finely minced fresh parsley

Dressing:
½ cup vegetable oil *or* ¼ cup each vegetable oil and olive oil
3 tablespoons fresh lemon juice
3 ounces Roquefort cheese, crumbled
¼ teaspoon freshly ground black pepper

Toss greens with scallions and parsley. Measure ingredients for dressing into a jar with a lid and shake well. This dressing will probably not need salt. If you like a smooth dressing, put in blender, but I prefer mine with the crumbled cheese showing.

CHOCOLATE ROYALE

4 ounces semi-sweet chocolate
3 tablespoons butter *or* margarine
¼ cup heavy cream
4 eggs, separated
2 tablespoons sugar
12 ladyfingers

Triple Sec sauce:
1 cup milk
¼ cup sugar
3 egg yolks
½ teaspoon vanilla
1 ounce Triple Sec *or* other orange-flavored liqueur

For cake filling, place chocolate, butter or margarine and cream into saucepan and melt over heat. Remove pan from heat and add **egg yolks,** stirring well with whisk. Over low heat, continue to stir until chocolate mixture thickens. Pour into a mixing bowl. Cool. Beat **egg whites** until soft peaks form, add sugar and beat until stiff. Fold ½ egg whites into chocolate with whisk. Add remaining whites, folding in with rubber spatula. Butter a 4½ x 8½-inch loaf pan and line with wax paper. Line sides of loaf pan with split ladyfingers. Pour chocolate mixture into loaf pan and refrigerate for 2 hours, then freeze. Remove from freezer and keep refrigerated 1 hour before serving. Slice and pour some sauce over each serving.

For sauce, place milk and sugar in saucepan over medium heat. Bring to boil. In medium-size mixing bowl, beat yolks and add hot milk slowly while stirring with whisk. Return mixture to saucepan and continue whisking over heat for several seconds. Sauce should thicken to coat a spoon. Do not boil. Add vanilla and liqueur. Cool and refrigerate, covered.

Serves 6

CONSOMMÉ DE MER • CHICKEN RONSARD
ALMOND NOODLES • FRENCH-STYLE GREEN BEANS
REFRIGERATOR ROLLS
CURACAO-ORANGE SHERBET WITH CHOCOLATE SAUCE

"An unusual blend of chicken breasts and vegetables. As a matter of fact, the whole menu is rather different and very pleasing."

CHICKEN RONSARD

3 tablespoons butter *or* margarine
3 tablespoons vegetable oil
3 large whole chicken breasts, skinned, boned and halved
All-purpose flour
Salt and pepper
½ cup coarsely grated onion
2 cloves garlic, minced
1 cup coarsely grated carrot
1 large tomato, peeled, seeded and chopped
½ cup canned chicken broth
1 cup dry vermouth
1 cup heavy cream
2 sprigs fresh parsley
1 bay leaf
¼ teaspoon dried thyme
1 tablespoon fresh tarragon, finely chopped *or* 1 teaspoon dried tarragon, crushed
1 celery rib

Heat butter or margarine and vegetable oil in large skillet until foaming subsides. Shape chicken breasts neatly and roll in flour, salt and pepper. Put into skillet and gently brown. Remove to plate. Add onion and garlic to skillet and sauté for 1 or 2 minutes. Add carrot, tomato, chicken broth and vermouth and heat until boiling. Add cream and stir 2 to 3 minutes.

Tie parsley, bay leaf, thyme, tarragon and celery in cheesecloth and add to vegetable mixture in skillet. Simmer gently for 30 minutes and remove garni. Season sauce with salt and pepper to taste.

Place chicken in a buttered casserole large enough to hold pieces in a single layer. Place vegetable sauce mixture over and around the chicken being certain the pieces of chicken are well surrounded. Cover and bake at 350° for ½ hour. Let chicken remain covered for a few minutes after removing from oven.

CONSOMMÉ DE MER

2 10½-ounce cans beef consommé (with gelatin added)
¼ cup tomato juice
3 tablespoons fresh lemon juice
2 tablespoons Worcestershire sauce
Salt and white pepper to taste
½ cup finely minced celery
½ cup crab meat or shrimp, drained and chopped
1 tablespoon mayonnaise
1 tablespoon dry Madeira wine (optional)
Few drops fresh lemon juice

Mix first 5 ingredients and chill until jelled. In another bowl, mix celery and either chopped crab meat or shrimp. Add the mayonnaise, the optional Madeira, and a few drops of lemon juice. Mix well and chill. Place a portion of seafood mixture in the bottom of each chilled soup bowl and cover with jellied consommé. Place a dot of additional mayonnaise on top of each serving, if desired.

ALMOND NOODLES

1 16-ounce package egg noodles
4 tablespoons butter *or* margarine
½ cup slivered almonds

Prepare egg noodles according to package instructions. Drain and butter with 2 tablespoons butter or margarine. In small skillet, add 2 tablespoons butter or margarine and slivered almonds; sauté for 1 or 2 minutes until butter or margarine and nuts are golden. Pour over noodles and mix well by tossing.

Note: To cook noodles ahead, after draining add 2 tablespoons vegetable oil and toss, coating all noodles. Just before serving, plunge noodles into boiling water for a few seconds to heat. Drain, then add butter or margarine and almonds.

REFRIGERATOR ROLLS

1 package active dry yeast
¼ cup lukewarm water (110°)
3 eggs
½ cup butter *or* margarine, melted
½ cup sugar
1 teaspoon salt
1 cup warm water
4½ cups all-purpose flour, sifted

Dissolve yeast in the ¼ cup lukewarm water. Beat eggs together, add melted butter or margarine, sugar, salt, yeast and the 1 cup water and flour. Mix and beat well. Mix the night before and let rise until doubled in bulk. Punch down. The dough will be sticky. Cover and put in refrigerator until ready to put in pans the next day.

Remove from refrigerator; shape into balls. Put in greased pans and let rise approximately 3 hours or until double in bulk. Bake at 375° about 10 minutes.

Note: These may be baked in the morning and reheated in foil in a 375° oven until warm.

FRENCH-STYLE GREEN BEANS

2 10-ounce packages frozen French-cut green beans
2 tablespoons butter *or* margarine
¼ cup minced scallions

Prepare French-cut green beans according to directions, keeping them nice and crisp-tender. Sauté 1 minute in butter or margarine, add minced scallions and toss.

CURACAO-ORANGE SHERBET WITH CHOCOLATE SAUCE

"Use a quart of sherbet and use left-over another time, it's so good."

1 quart orange sherbet, softened
4 tablespoons Curacao *or* other orange-flavored liqueur
Grated rind from 1 orange
4 oranges, peeled and sliced
1 cup rich chocolate sauce (your own or use a good brand)

In a bowl, let sherbet soften a bit, then beat in the liqueur and the grated orange peel. Return to freezer until ready to use. Peel oranges and be sure to cut down far enough to remove white pith, then slice in fairly thin slices. Sprinkle with a bit more liqueur and refrigerate.

To assemble, on each dessert plate, put 3 slices of orange and 2 small scoops of sherbet on top. Pour some of the chocolate sauce over the sherbet and fruit.

Italian Dinner Serves 12

BAGNA CAUDA DIP • SPAGHETTI
ARTICHOKE AND SHRIMP SAUCE
PESTO SAUCE • TOMATO MEAT SAUCE
ORANGE, ONION AND GREENS SALAD • CASSATA

"To make a fun, do-it-yourself party, let your guests choose the sauce they prefer or perhaps they will like a little of each."

SPAGHETTI

Make your own pasta or use packaged spaghetti. Plan on 1 pound of spaghetti to serve 4 to 6 people. The pasta can be cooked and stored for later use. To do this, cook and drain quickly, coat with 1 tablespoon vegetable oil and refrigerate in a tightly covered container. To use, place in a pot of boiling water just long enough to heat through. Drain and use immediately.

BAGNA CAUDA DIP

"Let your guests dip their choices of vegetables or bread cubes into the warm sauce on fondue forks."

1 cup butter *or* margarine
⅔ cup olive oil
2 2-ounce cans flat anchovy filets, drained and finely chopped
1 tablespoon finely chopped garlic
¼ teaspoon pepper
1½ cups dairy sour cream

Heat butter or margarine and olive oil in a saucepan over medium heat until butter foams. Add anchovies and garlic, cook and stir for 4 to 5 minutes; add pepper. Remove from heat and gradually stir in the sour cream. Heat but do not boil. Pour into a chafing dish and keep warm. Stir occasionally.

Serve with assorted vegetables such as cauliflower, artichoke hearts, cucumber, zucchini, carrot and celery sticks. Cubes of French bread may also be used.

ORANGE, ONION AND GREENS SALAD

1 tablespoon butter *or* margarine
½ cup coarsely chopped walnuts
¼ teaspoon salt
1½ pounds spinach leaves, torn
2 heads Bibb lettuce
1 cucumber, peeled or unpeeled, thinly sliced
4 oranges, peeled, thinly sliced, seeded and drained (reserve juice)
1 small red onion, sliced and separated into rings

Dressing:
½ cup vegetable oil
¼ cup orange juice
2 tablespoons cider vinegar
1½ teaspoons sugar
¼ teaspoon salt
¼ teaspoon freshly ground black pepper

Melt the butter or margarine in a small skillet over medium heat; add walnuts and sauté until crisp and slightly browned. Remove from heat and toss with the ¼ teaspoon salt. Set aside. Wash, drain and tear spinach and lettuce.

Toss the orange, cucumber, spinach, lettuce and onion together in a large glass salad bowl. Cover and store in the refrigerator as long as 4 hours.

For dressing, measure all ingredients into a jar with a lid and shake well, or put in the blender. Cover and refrigerate several hours. Just before serving time, add the walnuts and dressing to the orange and greens mixture. Toss.

ARTICHOKE AND SHRIMP SAUCE

⅓ cup chopped bacon
¼ cup chopped onion
2 tablespoons butter *or* margarine
1 cup heavy cream
1 9-ounce package frozen artichoke hearts, thawed and cut in quarters
½ cup canned tomatoes, undrained and chopped
1 teaspoon dried marjoram, crumbled
½ teaspoon salt
⅛ teaspoon freshly ground black pepper
¼ teaspoon ground nutmeg
4 ounces cooked small shrimp
Hot cooked pasta
Grated Parmesan cheese

In saucepan, sauté bacon and onion in butter or margarine over medium heat until bacon is barely crisp. Stir in all the other ingredients except shrimp, pasta and Parmesan cheese. Simmer uncovered until artichokes are tender and sauce is thickened. At this point, you may store sauce in refrigerator as long as 6 to 8 hours. Before serving, stir shrimp into the artichoke mixture. Heat until hot. Serve sauce over hot pasta. Pass Parmesan cheese.

PESTO SAUCE

2 cups fresh spinach leaves (pack leaves in cup)
¼ cup chopped fresh parsley
3 tablespoons toasted pine nuts *or* coarsely chopped, toasted walnuts
2 cloves garlic, chopped
2 teaspoons dried basil leaves, crumbled
½ teaspoon salt
¾ cup olive oil
¾ cup freshly grated Parmesan cheese
3 tablespoons butter *or* margarine, softened
Hot cooked pasta

Put spinach, parsley, nuts, garlic, basil and salt in a blender; pour in olive oil, cover and blend about 20 seconds. Push mixture down from the sides of the blender with a rubber spatula. Cover and blend about 25 seconds more until smooth. Turn into a bowl and stir in Parmesan cheese and softened butter or margarine. Serve sauce at room temperature over hot cooked pasta.

Note: This sauce can be made the day before. To double recipe, blend mixture in 2 batches.

TOMATO MEAT SAUCE

"This is a good recipe to make in a slow cooker."

1½ pounds ground beef
1 medium onion, chopped
1 1-pound can Italian tomatoes
1 15-ounce can tomato sauce
1 12-ounce can tomato paste
1 10¾-ounce can tomato soup
1 4-ounce can mushroom stems and pieces, with liquid
4 tablespoons chopped fresh parsley *or* 2 tablespoons dried parsley flakes
1 tablespoon Italian seasoning
1 tablespoon dried oregano
1 teaspoon dried basil leaves
1 teaspoon salt
¼ teaspoon minced garlic
Dash pepper
Hot cooked pasta
Grated Parmesan cheese

Sauté and stir ground beef and onion in large skillet until meat is brown and onion is tender. Drain off excess fat. Stir in remaining ingredients except hot cooked pasta and cheese. Cover; simmer 2 to 5 hours, stirring sauce occasionally. Serve over hot pasta; sprinkle with Parmesan cheese.

Note: Sauce can be eaten after 2 hours of simmering, but has a heartier Italian flavor when simmered a longer time. Can be made 2 days in advance.

CASSATA

1½ quarts vanilla ice cream, slightly softened
1 quart chocolate ice cream, slightly softened
½ cup heavy cream
1 teaspoon vanilla
1 egg white
2 tablespoons confectioners' sugar
2 tablespoons chopped candied red cherries
2 tablespoons chopped candied citron
2 tablespoons chopped candied orange peel
½ cup heavy cream
Whole candied red cherries

Line a 2-quart mold with vanilla ice cream. Freeze until firm, then cover vanilla ice cream with chocolate ice cream. Freeze until firm. Whip ½ cup of cream until stiff and blend in vanilla. Whip egg white to a soft peak, then beat in confectioners' sugar until stiff. Fold egg white into cream mixture, also the chopped cherries, citron and orange peel. Spoon this into center of molded ice cream and spread it to make a smooth layer. Cover and freeze. You may store this as long as a week in the freezer.

To unmold, dip the mold to the rim in hot water for a few seconds then invert onto a cold serving plate. Return to freezer to firm up the surface.

To serve, whip ½ cup heavy cream until stiff, use to decorate the Cassata and garnish with whole candied red cherries.

Serves 6

CLAMS ON THE SHELL • FLEMISH BEEF IN BEER
SPAETZLE • BUTTERED PARSLEY CARROTS
MOLDED BEET SALAD
SESAME TOAST • CREME DE CACAO PIE

"Here are some pleasant accompaniments to a favorite Flemish dish. The spicy tart flavor of the Molded Beet Salad is especially good."

CLAMS ON THE SHELL

3 6½-ounce cans chopped clams, reserve juice
½ cup chopped celery
¼ cup chopped onion
½ cup chopped green pepper
3 tablespoons butter *or* margarine
2 tablespoons all-purpose flour
¾ teaspoon salt
¼ teaspoon dried thyme, crushed
Dash Tabasco® pepper sauce
3 eggs, beaten
4 tablespoons dry vermouth
1 cup soft bread crumbs
2 tablespoons snipped fresh parsley
3 tablespoons heavy cream
½ cup saltine cracker crumbs
2 tablespoons butter *or* margarine, melted
Paprika

Carefully pour juice off chopped clams into small container. Let juice settle, then pour into cup leaving the sediment and possible chips of shell behind. Set aside.

In skillet, sauté celery, onion and green pepper in 3 tablespoons butter or margarine until tender. Blend in flour, salt, thyme and pepper sauce, stirring to mix well. Beat eggs and stir in clam juice and vermouth. Add this mixture into vegetables in skillet, stirring constantly until thickened. Fold in clams and bread crumbs, then parsley and cream. Remove from heat. Spoon mixture into 6 buttered shells (custard cups or a shallow casserole). Combine cracker crumbs with 2 tablespoons melted butter or margarine and sprinkle over clam mixture. Dust top with paprika, bake at 400° until browned and bubbly, about 15 to 20 minutes.

BUTTERED PARSLEY CARROTS

1½ pounds carrots, scraped and thinly sliced
½ cup water
Salt to taste
1 teaspoon sugar
1 tablespoon butter *or* margarine
Pepper to taste
2 tablespoons finely chopped fresh parsley

In saucepan with tight fitting lid, put carrots and about ½ cup water, salt and sugar. Cover and steam over low heat until tender, about 40 minutes. Take care not to scorch. Add butter or margarine, pepper and parsley. Toss and serve.

FLEMISH BEEF IN BEER

2 pounds sirloin steak, cut in ¼-inch strips
4 tablespoons butter *or* margarine
4 tablespoons vegetable oil
5 large onions, thinly sliced
Salt and pepper
4 cloves garlic, minced
¼ teaspoon dried thyme
2 tablespoons firmly packed brown sugar
1 10½-ounce can beef broth
1½ cups beer
1 bay leaf
2 tablespoons cornstarch
Fresh parsley

Brown meat in 2 tablespoons each of butter or margarine and vegetable oil. Remove meat. Add remaining vegetable oil and butter or margarine to skillet; add onions, season with sprinkle of salt and pepper. Sauté for 10 minutes. Put beef, onions and minced garlic in casserole in layers. Sprinkle with thyme and brown sugar. Heat ½ beef broth and 1½ cups beer in skillet used to brown meat, adding the bay leaf. Pour over beef, bring to boil on stove top, then bake in the covered casserole in 325° oven for 2½ hours. Remove meat to dish. Mix remaining beef broth with cornstarch; add to sauce in casserole and stir and simmer until thickened. Remove bay leaf. Return meat to sauce and heat for 5 minutes before serving. Garnish with parsley.

MOLDED BEET SALAD

1 1-pound can shoe string *or* cubed beets, reserve juice
1 3-ounce package lemon-flavored gelatin
⅓ cup sugar
⅛ teaspoon salt
1½ tablespoons mustard seeds
4 tablespoons cider vinegar
1 cup finely chopped celery
1 tablespoon grated onion
Mayonnaise

Drain beets, add enough water to beet juice to make 1 cup. Heat juice to boiling in saucepan, add gelatin, sugar, salt and mustard seeds and stir away from heat until gelatin is dissolved. Add vinegar, mix well and cool. Refrigerate. When thickened, add celery, beets and onions. Pour into an attractive mold or into individual molds. Refrigerate until firm. Top with mayonnaise.

SESAME TOAST

¾ cup butter *or* margarine
1 clove garlic, whole
¼ teaspoon dried thyme
Salt and pepper to taste
1 loaf of French bread
½ cup sesame seeds

In saucepan, melt butter or margarine with the clove of garlic. Add thyme and salt and pepper to taste. Let simmer for 2 or 3 minutes, then set aside to cool. Remove garlic. Cut loaf of bread into ¾-inch slices and dip slices into butter.

Spread sesame seeds on a sheet of wax paper. Roll bread crusts in the seeds, then sprinkle 1 side of each with seeds. Put slices, seeded side up, on a baking sheet. Bake in middle of a preheated 400° oven for 20 to 25 minutes or until they are lightly toasted and crisp. Arrange toast on a breadboard for serving.

SPAETZLE (LITTLE DUMPLINGS)

3 cups all-purpose flour
3 eggs
¾ teaspoon salt
¼ teaspoon black pepper
¼ teaspoon ground nutmeg
1 cup water, approximately
3 quarts boiling water with
2 teaspoons salt added
1 tablespoon butter *or* margarine

Sift flour into bowl, make a depression in the center and break into it 3 eggs. Add salt, pepper and nutmeg and about ¾ cup of the water. Mix this well (it should be a medium batter); if not soft enough, add water by drops until of the right consistency. Beat batter only until it is smooth. Pour batter into colander with large holes and with back of large spoon, force dough directly into 3 quarts salted boiling water. Stir gently to keep from sticking together. When the spaetzle rise to the surface, they are cooked. Drain and toss the spaetzle with 1 tablespoon butter or margarine to serve.

Note: Prepared, dried spaetzle may be purchased from gourmet sections in most food markets.

CREME DE CACAO PIE

1 quart vanilla ice cream, softened
⅓ cup creme de cacao
⅓ cup creme de menthe (green)
½ cup heavy cream, whipped
1 tablespoon confectioners' sugar
Semi-sweet chocolate

In a 10-inch glass, ovenproof pie pan, press down about a 1-inch-thick layer of vanilla ice cream. Spoon over it ½ of the creme de cacao, then cover with thinner layer of ice cream and cover with ½ amount of creme de menthe. Finish ice cream and liqueurs in the next 2 layers. Whip cream, adding confectioners' sugar, and spread a thin layer of this in swirls over the top of the pie. A few curls of chocolate would add a finishing touch, if you wish. Put in freezer to firm. Remove a few minutes before serving so that it will be easy to slice.

Greek Dinner Serves 6

CHILLED EGG-LEMON SOUP • MOUSSAKA
GREEK VEGETABLE SALAD
MEDITERRANEAN RICE PUDDING

"Moussaka is rich and very good. It is best to use lamb. However, beef may be substituted for the lamb if you wish. The feta cheese in the salad is particularly tasty."

MOUSSAKA

2 medium eggplants, sliced into ½-inch rounds
Vegetable oil
¾ cup bread crumbs
3 tablespoons butter *or* margarine
3 tablespoons all-purpose flour
1½ cups milk, heated to boiling
2 egg yolks, well beaten
1 cup creamed cottage cheese
1½ pounds ground lamb from shoulder (fat, gristle removed)
1½ medium onions, chopped
½ cup Burgundy wine
2 tablespoons tomato paste
Salt and pepper
⅛ teaspoon garlic powder
¼ cup chopped fresh parsley
½ cup grated Parmesan cheese
1 cup grated Monterey Jack *or* mozzarella cheese

Peel eggplant and slice into rounds. Dip slices in vegetable oil and lay on broiler pan. Broil, about 6 to 8 inches under heat on each side until lightly browned. (This may necessitate 2 or 3 batches.) Grease an 8½ x 13-inch rectangular casserole dish and cover bottom with ¼ cup of the bread crumbs. Add a layer of eggplant.

Melt butter or margarine in saucepan. Add flour and cook over medium heat 3 to 4 minutes. Add hot milk and continue cooking until thickened, stirring constantly. Add 1 cup of the hot mixture to beaten yolks then quickly stir into rest of sauce. Cook 3 minutes longer, stirring constantly. Remove from heat and cool sauce. Stir in cottage cheese. Brown lamb in a little vegetable oil with onions. Add Burgundy wine, simmer a minute, then add tomato paste, salt and pepper, garlic and parsley.

To casserole dish with layer of eggplant, add layer of meat mixture. Sprinkle with ¼ cup of the remaining bread crumbs and ¼ cup grated Parmesan cheese. Repeat layers. Pour sauce over the top and cover with foil. Bake in 350° oven for 45 minutes, then remove foil and sprinkle grated Monterey Jack or mozzarella cheese over the top and continue cooking for another 15 minutes. Let rest 10 minutes before cutting to serve.

CHILLED EGG-LEMON SOUP

3 cups canned chicken broth
2 tablespoons + 1 teaspoon cornstarch
1⅓ cups heavy cream
6 egg yolks
2 whole eggs
4 tablespoons fresh lemon juice
Salt and white pepper
Grated peel of 1 lemon

Heat the chicken broth. In small bowl, dissolve cornstarch in cream and slowly add to broth, stirring constantly over low heat until smooth and thickened. Beat yolks and whole eggs until thick and lemony; slowly add lemon juice, while beating constantly. Pour broth and cream slowly into egg mix. Stir well and return to low heat for 3 to 4 minutes, stirring constantly, until soup thickens. Salt and pepper to taste. Be careful of curdling by overheating. Cool and chill. Serve in small chilled cups garnished with the grated lemon peel.

GREEK VEGETABLE SALAD

Use all or some of the following ingredients for the salad: Tear several kinds of greens into bite-size pieces. Add sliced cucumber, chopped green onions (or sliced red or white onion), shredded red cabbage, green pepper strips, tomato wedges, shredded carrots, celery strips, sliced radishes, pitted ripe olives, young tender raw zucchini strips, crumbled feta cheese, chopped parsley. Season with salt, pepper and oregano, finely crushed and sprinkled over the vegetables. Top with anchovy filets. Toss well.

Dressing:
2 parts olive oil
1 part wine vinegar or fresh lemon juice
Sprinkle of garlic powder
Salt and pepper

Measure ingredients for dressing into a jar with a lid and shake well, or put in the blender. Pour over salad and toss well.

MEDITERRANEAN RICE PUDDING

½ cup raw long-grain white rice
1 quart milk
1 egg, separated
½ cup sugar
3 tablespoons half-and-half
1 teaspoon vanilla
Ground cinnamon

In saucepan, bring rice and milk to boil, then lower heat and cook approximately 40 minutes or until rice is tender. Beat **egg white** until stiff, then beat in ¼ cup sugar, 1 tablespoon at a time, until egg white forms stiff peaks. In small bowl, beat **egg yolk** with the remaining sugar until light in color and very thick. Beat in half-and-half. Fold egg white into yolk mixture. Add to rice and cook over moderate heat, stirring for 5 to 7 minutes; add vanilla. Put in bowls and sprinkle cinnamon on top. Serve either warm or cold.

Serves 8

STUFFED LEG OF LAMB BELLE HÉLÈNE
or
ROAST LEG OF LAMB • MINT SAUCE
SPINACH RING MEDLEY • CREAMED ONIONS
HARVARD BEETS • MACARONI-CHEESE LOAF
BROWNIE PIE

"So good – with a lot of eye appeal. If you are doing this for guests I would suggest that you make sure all of your guests like lamb. It can be a problem as there are quite a few people who just don't like lamb. In that case baked ham could be used as a substitute."

STUFFED LEG OF LAMB BELLE HÉLÈNE

2 tablespoons butter *or* margarine
2 tablespoons minced scallions
1 clove garlic, minced
1 tablespoon minced celery
2 tablespoons finely minced pork fat (if salted, blanch in boiling water)
1 tart apple, peeled, seeded and chopped medium-fine
¾ cup toasted bread crumbs (very dry)
1 tablespoon minced fresh parsley
¼ teaspoon dried rosemary, finely crushed
1 teaspoon fresh lemon juice
2 eggs, well beaten
Salt and pepper
1 5- to 6-pound leg of lamb (have the butcher bone the leg)
Vegetable oil

For the stuffing, melt butter or margarine and sauté scallions, garlic and celery with minced pork fat in a skillet. Add apple and sauté 4 to 5 minutes. Toss in bread crumbs, parsley, rosemary and lemon juice. Remove from heat after mixing well. Let cool and add eggs; mix well. Sprinkle with salt and pepper to taste. Rub area where lamb bone was removed with salt and pepper and a pinch of finely crushed rosemary.

Put stuffing in the area where bone was removed, and using skewers and string, shape the leg into a neat, rounded loaf. Salt and pepper outside liberally after rubbing with vegetable oil. Bake in shallow roasting pan at 350° for about 1½ hours or until meat thermometer registers 160°. Let rest for 15 minutes after removing from oven before carving. Keep warm on open oven door or in another warm place. Slice and serve with degreased pan juices.

ROAST LEG OF LAMB (WITH BONE IN)

1 5- to 6-pound leg of lamb
Clove garlic, minced
Vegetable oil
1 teaspoon dried rosemary, finely crushed
Salt and pepper

At various places just under the fat, slash and place bits of garlic (also close to the bone) using as much as you like. Rub over the outside as well. Rub vegetable oil over outside of the leg. Rub in the rosemary, then sprinkle liberally with salt and pepper. Roast in 350° oven until meat thermometer registers 160° for a slightly pink, juicy piece of meat. (If meat is overcooked, it becomes gray and dry.) Let roast rest for 15 minutes after removing from oven to facilitate carving and minimize loss of juices.

MINT SAUCE

"A favorite with lamb as well as pork."

1 10-ounce jar red currant jelly
1 cup + 2 tablespoons chili sauce
¼ cup liquid mint sauce

Combine red currant jelly and chili sauce in small saucepan. Over low heat, stir until jelly is melted and mixture is well-blended. Add mint sauce, blend and heat through. This makes about 2⅓ cups sauce.

MACARONI-CHEESE LOAF

Grated Parmesan cheese
1 8-ounce package elbow macaroni
1½ cups milk
2 tablespoons butter *or* margarine
½ onion, chopped
1½ cups shredded sharp Cheddar cheese
1 teaspoon salt
⅛ teaspoon pepper
¼ teaspoon dried marjoram
3 large eggs
Paprika
Sliced stuffed green olives

Butter and sprinkle loaf pan with grated Parmesan cheese. Cook macaroni according to package instructions. Drain. In saucepan, heat milk, add butter or margarine, onions, Cheddar cheese, salt, pepper and marjoram. Beat eggs and stir into the milk mixture. Mix into the cooked macaroni. Pour into prepared 9⅝ x 5½ x 2¾-inch loaf pan and bake at 325° for 45 minutes, or until firm. Let stand 10 minutes and unmold. Garnish wth sprinkle of paprika and slices of stuffed green olives, if desired.

SPINACH RING MEDLEY

2 10-ounce packages frozen chopped spinach, cooked, drained (reserve water)
3 tablespoons butter *or* margarine
3 tablespoons all-purpose flour
Spinach water + milk to make ¾ cup liquid
½ teaspoon salt
¼ teaspoon pepper
¼ teaspoon ground nutmeg
3 eggs, beaten

Cook spinach according to package directions and drain well, reserving spinach water. Melt butter or margarine in saucepan, add flour and mix to smooth paste. Add spinach water plus milk to make ¾ cup of liquid. Simmer sauce for a few minutes. Add seasonings and the spinach. Fold in beaten eggs and pour mixture into well buttered 1½-quart ring mold. Set in pan of hot water and bake at 375° for 1 hour or until the center is firm. Unmold and fill the center with the Creamed Onions and surround with Harvard Beets (see following recipes).

CREAMED ONIONS

1 pound small fresh or frozen onions, *or* if not available, larger yellow onions can be cut in eighths
2 tablespoons butter *or* margarine
2 tablespoons all-purpose flour
1 cup evaporated milk *or* 1 cup half-and-half
¼ cup liquid from steaming onions
Salt and pepper to taste
2 tablespoons dairy sour cream

Steam onions and reserve steaming water to add to the sauce. There should be about ¼ cup liquid. (If the larger yellow onions are used, they will retain their shape to a great extent if some of the root end is left intact when cut into eighths.) Melt butter or margarine in saucepan and stir in flour. Let simmer 2 to 3 minutes. Add milk and the water from onions gradually, and whisk to remove any lumps. Cook about 7 to 8 minutes. Add salt and pepper to taste. Add sour cream and the onions. Keep hot; pour in center of Spinach Ring Medley just before serving.

HARVARD BEETS

½ cup sugar
1 tablespoon cornstarch
½ teaspoon salt
½ cup cider vinegar
2 whole cloves
2 tablespoons butter *or* margarine
2 1-pound cans small whole beets

In saucepan stir sugar, cornstarch, salt, vinegar and cloves. Cook and stir until clear. Add butter or margarine and beets. Stir until beets are hot. May be made ahead and heated just before serving. Put the beets around the outside of the Spinach Ring Medley just before serving.

BROWNIE PIE

3 egg whites
Dash of salt
¼ teaspoon cream of tartar
¾ cup granulated sugar
¾ cup finely crushed chocolate wafer crumbs (14 wafers)
¾ cup chopped black walnuts
½ teaspoon vanilla
2 tablespoons confectioners' sugar
1 cup heavy cream, whipped, *or* vanilla ice cream

Beat egg whites until foamy and add salt and cream of tartar. Continue to beat until peaks form. Add sugar to whites, 2 tablespoons at a time, and continue to beat until stiff and glossy. Fold in wafer crumbs and black walnuts. Fold in vanilla. Butter a 10-inch glass pie pan and sprinkle with granulated sugar. Pour in the mixture and smooth the top. Bake about 45 minutes at 325°. Let cool completely in oven. Spread with whipped cream sweetened with confectioners' sugar and refrigerate until ready to serve. You may prefer to serve with scoops of vanilla ice cream instead.

Serves 6

POLYNESIAN CHICKEN • OVEN BAKED RICE
OVEN STEAMED CARROTS
ZUCCHINI WITH FRESH HERBS
TOMATO ASPIC • BANANA NUT TORTE

"Here is a menu that will appeal to both young and old. Most children like the sweet-sour flavor of Polynesian cooking."

OVEN STEAMED CARROTS

1½ pounds carrots, scraped and thinly sliced
3 tablespoons butter *or* margarine
3 tablespoons water
3 tablespoons dry white wine (optional)
1 teaspoon sugar
Salt and white pepper

On top of stove in saucepan, place sliced carrots, butter or margarine, water, optional wine, sugar and a couple of grinds of white pepper and salt to taste. Bring to boil. Butter shallow casserole with tightly fitting lid. Transfer boiling carrots to casserole and put into 350° oven to cook for approximately 1 hour. Carrots should be crisp-tender.

Note: These can cook at the same time as the rest of the dinner.

POLYNESIAN CHICKEN

12 large chicken thighs
½ cup all-purpose flour
⅓ cup vegetable oil
1 teaspoon salt
¼ teaspoon pepper

Sauce:
1 20-ounce can sliced pineapple, reserve juice
1 cup sugar
2 tablespoons cornstarch
¾ cup cider vinegar
1 tablespoon soy sauce
¼ teaspoon ground ginger
1 chicken bouillon cube
1 large green pepper, sliced crosswise into ¼-inch circles

Coat chicken with flour; brown in skillet in hot vegetable oil. Remove, as browned, to shallow roasting pan, arranging pieces skin side up. Sprinkle with salt and pepper. Preheat oven to 350°.

To make sauce, drain pineapple, pouring syrup into 2-cup measure. Add water to make 1½ cups. In medium-size saucepan, combine sugar, cornstarch, pineapple syrup, vinegar, soy sauce, ginger and bouillon cube. Bring to boil, stirring constantly. Boil 2 minutes; pour sauce over chicken. Bake uncovered 30 minutes. Add pineapple slices and green pepper, bake 15 minutes longer, or until chicken is tender. Serve with Oven Baked Rice (recipe follows).

Note: This dish can be made ahead up to baking and held in refrigerator overnight. One hour before baking, remove from refrigerator. Bake 45 minutes and add pineapple and green pepper, continue to bake for 15 minutes. If you have real hearty eaters, prepare more chicken pieces. Additional sauce is not necessary.

OVEN BAKED RICE

1 cup raw long-grain white rice
2½ cups hot water
½ teaspoon salt

Toast rice in skillet over medium heat, shaking often, about 10 minutes. Turn into 1-quart casserole; add hot water and salt, stirring to separate. Cover and bake in 350° oven for 1 hour or until rice is tender and water has been absorbed. Fluff rice with fork.

Note: This can be baked in the same oven while cooking the Polynesian Chicken.

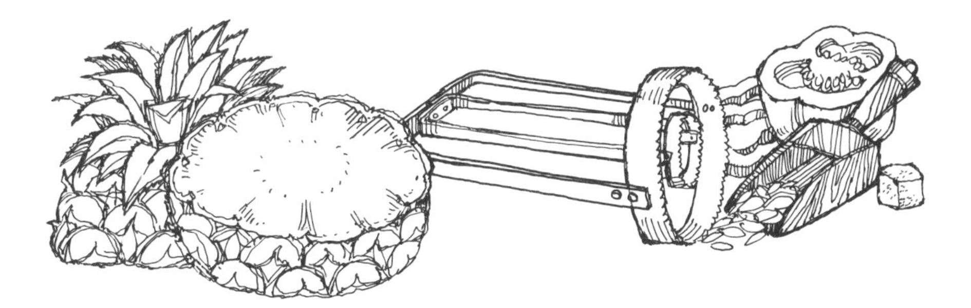

ZUCCHINI WITH FRESH HERBS

8 small zucchini (about 2 pounds)
¼ cup water
½ teaspoon salt
¼ teaspoon freshly ground black pepper
¼ cup butter *or* margarine, melted
2 tablespoons finely chopped fresh parsley
1 tablespoon minced chives *or* 1 teaspoon dried dill weed
1 tablespoon fresh lemon juice

Wash zucchini, remove stem and flowered end. Cut into diagonal, ¼-inch-thick slices. In medium-size skillet with tight-fitting lid, bring water with salt and pepper to boil. Add zucchini and cook over medium-low heat, covered, for 10 minutes or until just crisp-tender (water should be nearly evaporated). Turn up heat to evaporate liquid, taking care not to scorch. Add butter or margarine, parsley, chives or dill weed and lemon juice, tossing gently to coat vegetable. Turn into heated serving dish.

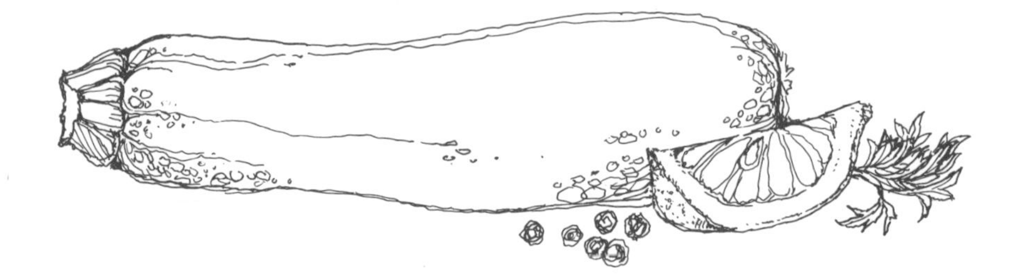

BANANA NUT TORTE

"For a change, substitute the bananas with fresh peaches or strawberries sweetened, if necessary."

1 cup granulated sugar
1 teaspoon baking powder
3 egg whites, at room temperature
12 saltine crackers, finely crushed
⅔ cup chopped walnuts
1 teaspoon vanilla

Topping:
2 to 3 ripe bananas
1 cup heavy cream, whipped
2 tablespoons confectioners' sugar
1 teaspoon vanilla
½ cup chopped walnuts

Sift sugar with baking powder. In another bowl, beat egg whites until fairly stiff. Add sugar mixture, 2 tablespoons at a time, beating constantly. Fold in saltines, ⅔ cup walnuts and 1 teaspoon vanilla. Spread evenly in well-buttered 9- or 10-inch round pan. Bake in preheated 350° oven 20 to 25 minutes. The torte will not be brown on top. Leave in oven until cool, then remove. (This much can be done a day ahead.)

Slice bananas generously over top of torte. Whip cream, adding confectioners' sugar and 1 teaspoon of vanilla. Beat until firm. Spread cream over bananas, covering thoroughly. Sprinkle ½ cup chopped walnuts on top. Refrigerate until ready to serve. Cut in wedges.

TOMATO ASPIC

"If you are using a ring mold, why not fill the center with cottage cheese in which you've mixed chopped chives, cucumber, and a little chopped green pepper?"

1 3-ounce package lemon-flavored gelatin
¾ cup boiling water
1 10¾-ounce can tomato soup
2 tablespoons cider vinegar *or* fresh lemon juice
1 cup chopped celery
3 tablespoons chopped onion
¼ cup sliced stuffed green olives (optional)
Lettuce, washed, dried and chilled
Mayonnaise

Dissolve gelatin in boiling water, add soup and vinegar or lemon juice. Stir until well blended. Chill until slightly thick but not set. Add celery, onion and sliced olives and stir well. Pour into a 1-quart mold, ring mold or 6 individual molds. Chill until firm. Unmold on salad greens and serve with mayonnaise.

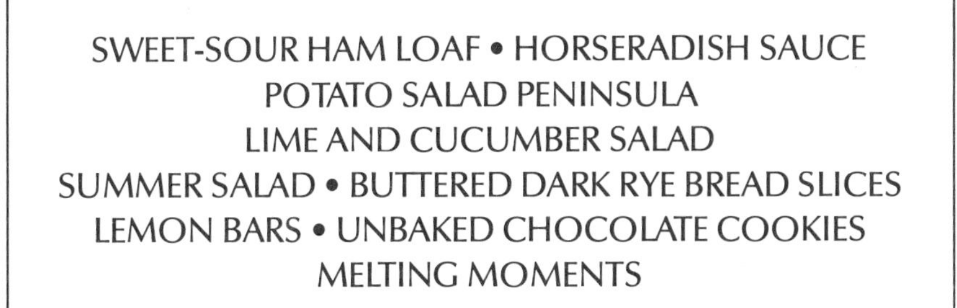

Patio Party Menu Serves 10

SWEET-SOUR HAM LOAF • HORSERADISH SAUCE
POTATO SALAD PENINSULA
LIME AND CUCUMBER SALAD
SUMMER SALAD • BUTTERED DARK RYE BREAD SLICES
LEMON BARS • UNBAKED CHOCOLATE COOKIES
MELTING MOMENTS

"A good menu for a large number of guests – to triple these recipes would not be difficult. The whole dinner can be eaten with a fork, which is an important consideration when you're serving many people."

LIME AND CUCUMBER SALAD

2 3-ounce packages lime-flavored gelatin
3½ cups boiling water
2 tablespoons cider vinegar
Dash of salt
2 tablespoons grated onion
2 large cucumbers, unpeeled and grated

Dissolve gelatin in boiling water, stir in vinegar, salt and onion. Put in refrigerator to thicken. Leave skin on cucumbers and grate. When gelatin thickens, fold in cucumber and turn into mold. Refrigerate until firm.

SWEET-SOUR HAM LOAF

2½ pounds smoked ham, ground (For better flavor, buy bone-in ham and have the butcher bone and grind the ham with the pork.)
½ pound ground pork
2 eggs, beaten
1 cup crushed saltine cracker crumbs
¼ teaspoon pepper
½ cup chopped onions
1 cup milk

Mustard glaze:
¾ cup firmly packed brown sugar
1½ tablespoons prepared mustard
3 tablespoons cider vinegar
2 tablespoons water

For ham loaf, mix all ingredients thoroughly. Form into a loaf and bake in a shallow pan. Bake at 350° for 2 hours.

For mustard glaze, blend well all ingredients and spread over ham loaf during last ½ hour of baking, basting often with sauce in the pan.

Horseradish Sauce: Serve with prepared cream style horseradish added to 1 cup dairy sour cream to taste.

BUTTERED DARK RYE BREAD SLICES

Either make your own or purchase from the bakery, a nice dark rye loaf. Butter, keeping loaf assembled, wrap in foil and heat in oven.

SUMMER SALAD

6 scallions, cut in ½-inch pieces
2 pounds carrots, thick sliced and cooked
1½ green peppers, sliced
1 cup sugar
¾ cup cider vinegar
1 10¾-ounce can tomato soup
½ cup vegetable oil
1 teaspoon prepared mustard
1 teaspoon Worcestershire sauce
Few grinds fresh pepper
Salt to taste

Prepare vegetables and put into large glass jar or covered refrigerator dish. Mix other ingredients and pour over vegetables assuring that all surfaces are covered. Let marinate in refrigerator for 24 hours before serving.

LEMON BARS

1 cup all-purpose flour
¼ cup confectioners' sugar
6 tablespoons butter *or* margarine, melted
2 eggs
1 cup granulated sugar
Juice of 1 medium lemon
2 tablespoons all-purpose flour
½ teaspoon baking powder
¼ teaspoon salt

Mix 1 cup flour with confectioners' sugar, add melted butter or margarine and press evenly into bottom of an 8-inch square pan. Bake for 20 minutes at 325°. Beat eggs, add granulated sugar and lemon juice, then 2 tablespoons flour, baking powder and salt. Beat together well and pour over crust. Bake about 30 minutes at 325°, then turn to 350° for last 5 minutes to give crust a delicate brown color.

To serve, sprinkle with confectioners' sugar and cut in squares.

POTATO SALAD PENINSULA

6 cups cubed russet potatoes, cooked
1⅓ cups chopped celery
1 onion, minced
2 teaspoons finely chopped fresh parsley
10 slices bacon, crisply fried and drained, reserve drippings
2 eggs, beaten
¼ cup sugar
¼ cup cider vinegar
¼ cup tarragon vinegar
1½ teaspoons salt
⅛ teaspoon pepper
⅛ teaspoon powdered savory
½ teaspoon dry mustard
¼ cup cold water
¼ cup bacon drippings
6 to 8 cups of assorted salad greens, washed, dried and chilled
4 tomatoes, chilled

Toss together potatoes, celery, onion and parsley. Crumble fried bacon into potato mixture. Set aside. In another bowl, mix the eggs, sugar, vinegars, salt, pepper and savory. Make a smooth paste with mustard and water and add to egg mixture. Pour into bacon drippings in skillet. Cook and stir until smooth and thickened. Add to potato mixture. Mix thoroughly. Cover and chill overnight or for 4 to 6 hours.

Serve mounded on bed of assorted salad greens garnished with tomato wedges.

UNBAKED CHOCOLATE COOKIES

1 12-ounce package chocolate chips
1 tablespoon butter *or* margarine
3 egg whites
½ teaspoon salt
⅛ teaspoon cream of tartar
1 cup confectioners' sugar
1 teaspoon vanilla
2 cups miniature marshmallows
1 cup walnuts, broken

In double boiler, melt chocolate chips over hot water with butter or margarine. In a bowl, beat egg whites until fluffy, add salt, continue beating a minute, add cream of tartar and beat until fairly stiff peaks form. Add confectioners' sugar 2 tablespoons at a time, continuing to beat until very stiff peaks form; add vanilla. Add chocolate mixture to egg whites. Fold marshmallows and walnuts into this mixture. Drop by spoonfuls on wax paper until set. Makes about 48.

MELTING MOMENTS

"So good . . . they just melt in your mouth."

1 cup real butter
5½ tablespoons granulated sugar
¾ cup corn starch
1 cup sifted all-purpose flour

Frosting:
¾ cup confectioners' sugar
1½ tablespoons fresh orange juice

Cream butter and sugar; add cornstarch and flour and mix well. Form into balls about the size of a nickel. Bake at 350° for 20 minutes or until firm to the touch. Cool.

For frosting, mix confectioners' sugar and orange juice. Frost top of each cookie.

Scandinavian Smorgasbord Serves 12

PICKLED HERRING • PICKLED BEETS
CUCUMBERS AND ONIONS IN SOUR CREAM
SWEDISH MEATBALLS • LAMB IN DILL SAUCE
SLICED COLD ROAST BEEF • SLICED COLD ROAST PORK
JANSSON'S TEMPTATION • BUTTERED PARSLEY POTATOES
SWEDISH BROWN BEANS
SWEET AND SOUR RED CABBAGE
CREAMED PEAS AND CARROTS IN TIMBALES
SWEDISH RYE BREAD
FRUIT BOWL WITH WHIPPED CREAM or SWEDISH CREAM
KRUMKAKE • SPRITZ • ROSETTES

"This kind of a party really impresses guests. Most dishes can be made the day before or even days before. The trick is getting it on the table all at once, I suggest you have help for that. Have salad plates for the first course of pickled herring, cucumbers and pickled beets."

JANSSON'S TEMPTATION

7 medium russet potatoes, peeled and cut into 2x¼-inch strips *or* into slices as for scalloped potatoes
3 tablespoons butter *or* margarine + 1 tablespoon butter *or* margarine for baking dish
2 tablespoons vegetable oil
3 large yellow onions, thinly sliced (about 4 cups)
16 flat anchovy filets, drained
White pepper
2 tablespoons fine dry bread crumbs
2 tablespoons butter *or* margarine, cut in ¼-inch bits
½ cup milk
1 cup heavy cream

Preheat oven to 400°. Place potato strips or slices in cold water to keep from discoloring. Heat 3 tablespoons butter or margarine and 2 tablespoons vegetable oil in large skillet. Add onions and sauté 10 minutes, stirring, until they are soft but not brown. Spread 1 tablespoon butter or margarine in 2-quart, flat baking dish or soufflé dish. Arrange a layer of potatoes on bottom of dish and then alternate layers of onions and anchovies, ending with potatoes. Sprinkle each layer with a little white pepper. Scatter bread crumbs over top layer and dot top with ¼-inch pieces of butter or margarine. In small saucepan, heat milk and cream until barely simmering; pour over potatoes. Bake in center of oven for 45 minutes or until potatoes are tender when pierced with tip of sharp knife and liquid is nearly absorbed.

SLICED COLD ROAST BEEF
and
SLICED COLD ROAST PORK

Prepare roast beef and pork the day before, refrigerate. Bring to room temperature before serving.

PICKLED HERRING

The best pickled herring is imported from Norway and found in specialty shops in most shopping centers.

SWEET AND SOUR RED CABBAGE

- 4 tablespoons bacon drippings
- 8 cups shredded red cabbage
- 4 cups cubed apple, unpeeled
- ½ cup firmly packed brown sugar
- ½ cup cider vinegar
- 2½ teaspoons salt
- Dash pepper
- 1 teaspoon caraway seeds
- ½ cup water

Heat drippings in large skillet or Dutch oven; add remaining ingredients and ½ cup water. Cook covered, over low heat, stirring occasionally. For crisp cabbage, cook 15 minutes; for tender cabbage, cook 25 to 30 minutes.

Note: The cabbage may be made the day before then reheated before serving.

SWEDISH MEATBALLS

- 4 tablespoons butter *or* margarine
- 8 tablespoons finely chopped onion
- 2 large potatoes, boiled and mashed (about 2 cups)
- 6 tablespoons fine dry bread crumbs
- 2 pounds lean ground beef
- ⅔ cup heavy cream
- 2 eggs
- 2 tablespoons finely chopped fresh parsley (optional)
- 2 teaspoons salt
- 4 tablespoons butter *or* margarine
- 4 tablespoons vegetable oil
- 2 tablespoons all-purpose flour
- 1½ cups half-and-half *or* heavy cream

In small skillet, melt 4 tablespoons butter or margarine, add onion and sauté until transparent. In large bowl, combine onion, mashed potatoes, bread crumbs, meat, ⅔ cup heavy cream, eggs, parsley and salt. Knead vigorously with both hands until well blended and mixture is smooth and fluffy. Shape into small balls about 1-inch in diameter. Arrange meatballs in a baking dish or on a flat tray, cover and chill for at least 1 hour.

On high heat, melt 4 tablespoons butter or margarine and 4 tablespoons vegetable oil in a heavy skillet. Reduce heat and add meatballs; fry on all sides by shaking pan. Remove meatballs; pour off grease. Stir in flour and brown slightly. Add 1½ cups half-and-half or heavy cream and cook, stirring until sauce thickens. Return meatballs to skillet and heat well.

LAMB IN DILL SAUCE

4 pounds breast or shoulder of lamb, cut in 2-inch cubes
4 to 5 cups water
1 bay leaf
5 sprigs fresh parsley
5 sprigs fresh dill (if obtainable)
1 tablespoon salt
4 whole peppercorns, white if possible

Dill sauce:
2½ cups reduced lamb stock (from above)
2 tablespoons butter *or* margarine
2 tablespoons all-purpose flour
3 tablespoons chopped fresh dill *or* 1½ teaspoons dried dill weed
1 tablespoon white vinegar
2 teaspoons sugar
½ teaspoon salt
½ teaspoon fresh lemon juice
1 egg yolk, slightly beaten
Fresh dill sprigs *or* parsley
Lemon slices

In heavy casserole, cover lamb with water and bring to boil, uncovered. Lower heat and simmer 10 to 15 minutes. Skim off scum as it rises to surface. Add bouquet of bay leaf, parsley and dill tied together in cheesecloth. Add salt and peppercorns. Partially cover pot and simmer for 1½ hours or until meat is tender. Remove lamb and keep warm (covered).

For dill sauce, strain lamb stock through fine sieve and boil down rapidly until reduced to 2½ cups. In another saucepan, melt butter or margarine and stir in flour. Sauté 2 to 3 minutes. Add lamb stock all at once. While whisking, bring to boil and simmer 5 to 10 minutes until thick and smooth. Add dill, vinegar, sugar, salt and lemon juice. Stir in a couple tablespoons of the hot dill sauce to beaten egg yolk, then return mixture back to sauce, beating constantly with whisk. Heat through again, but do not let sauce boil. Taste for seasoning; add salt and pepper if necessary.

To serve, strain sauce over the lamb. Garnish the platter with parsley or sprigs of dill, if obtainable, and lemon slices.

CUCUMBERS AND ONIONS IN SOUR CREAM

4 medium cucumbers, thinly sliced
2 medium red onions, separated into rings
1⅓ cups dairy sour cream
2 tablespoons fresh lemon juice
1 teaspoon dry dill weed
Salt to taste

Mix the sliced cucumbers with the onion rings. Gently fold the sour cream, lemon juice and dill into the vegetables. Taste for salt. Chill thoroughly.

SWEDISH BROWN BEANS

6 slices bacon, chopped
3 1-pound cans kidney beans (pour off half liquid)
¾ cup firmly packed brown sugar, *or* to taste
¼ teaspoon ground cinnamon
¼ teaspoon ground nutmeg
3 tablespoons cider vinegar
Salt and pepper to taste

Sauté chopped bacon until tender. Pour off grease. Mix all ingredients together and simmer, covered, for 30 minutes.

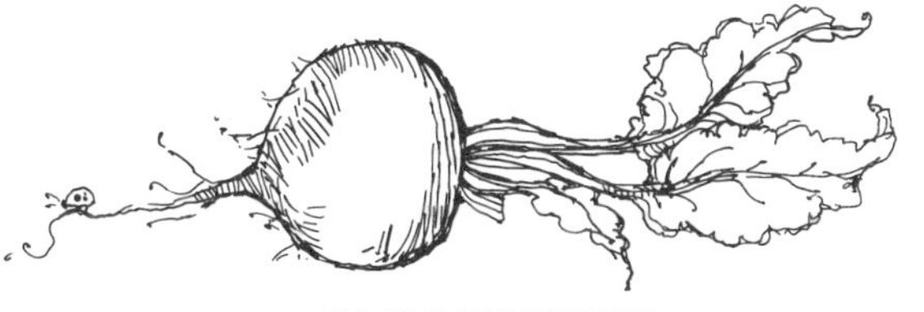

PICKLED BEETS

2 1-pound cans sliced beets *or* small whole beets
⅔ cup sugar
⅔ cup reserved beet liquid
⅔ cup cider vinegar
2 teaspoons pickling spices

Drain beets and reserve ⅔ cup liquid. In saucepan combine drained beets, sugar, reserved beet liquid and vinegar. Tie pickling spices in a piece of cheesecloth. Add to beets; cook until mixture comes to a boil. Cool and remove garni before serving. Will keep several weeks in the refrigerator.

Note: The same technique can be used with fresh cooked beets.

BUTTERED PARSLEY POTATOES

(See recipe for Buttered Parsley Potatoes included with French dinner menu on page 42.)

SWEDISH CREAM

2 envelopes unflavored gelatin
2 cups heavy cream
2 cups sugar
2 cups dairy sour cream
1 teaspoon vanilla
Sweetened fruit

In small saucepan, sprinkle gelatin on heavy cream to soften; add sugar. Stir over low heat until gelatin and sugar are dissolved. Do not let it boil. Remove from heat and chill until mixture begins to thicken. Add sour cream and vanilla to gelatin mixture, blending well. Pour into sherbet or parfait glasses and chill. Serve topped with sweetened fruit, such as strawberries or raspberries.

Note: The cream will keep for several days.

SWEDISH RYE BREAD

2¼ cups lukewarm water
2 cups rye flour
1 package dry yeast
¼ cup sugar
½ cup dark molasses
1½ teaspoons salt
¼ cup lard *or* solid vegetable shortening, melted
1 teaspoon caraway seeds
4 to 5 cups white all-purpose flour
Butter *or* margarine, melted

Stir 2 cups lukewarm water into rye flour; add yeast softened in ¼ cup lukewarm water. Mix well. Add sugar, dark molasses, salt, melted fat and caraway seeds. Add the white flour, kneading it in. Let rise to double in bulk. Punch down and make into loaves (should make 2 to 3 loaves). Put into greased pans and let rise again. Bake in 350° oven for 45 minutes to 1 hour. Remove from oven and brush tops of loaves with melted butter or margarine. Turn out on cake rack to cool.

CREAMED PEAS AND CARROTS IN TIMBALES

2 10-ounce packages frozen peas and carrots (mixed)
3 tablespoons + 1 teaspoon butter *or* margarine
3 tablespoons + 1 teaspoon all-purpose flour
2 cups milk
Salt and pepper to taste
12 timbale cases*

Cook peas and carrots according to package directions. Drain. In a saucepan, melt butter or margarine; add flour and cook the roux a few seconds, stirring constantly. Do not let it brown. Add milk; cook and stir until mixture thickens and bubbles. Add peas and carrots and season to taste with salt and pepper. At serving time, fill timbales with creamed peas and carrots.

***Note:** Timbales are paper thin patty shells made with batter from the Rosette recipe on page 83. They are formed with timbale irons (usually sold with rosette irons) and deep fried in the same manner. Timbales may be made days ahead and stored in an airtight container.

KRUMKAKE

"These golden cookies can be served flat or rolled and filled. You bake them in a special iron."

3 eggs
½ cup sugar
6 tablespoons butter *or* margarine, melted
½ teaspoon lemon extract
½ teaspoon ground cardamon (optional)
⅔ cup all-purpose flour, unsifted
Heavy cream, whipped

Beat eggs with all the ingredients except flour and heavy cream with electric mixer for 3 to 5 minutes. Blend in flour. To bake a cookie, place Krumkake iron directly over medium-high heat. Alternately heat both sides of iron until water dripped inside sizzles. Open and brush iron lightly with melted butter or margarine. For each cookie, spoon about 1 tablespoon batter into center of a buttered 5-inch iron (about 1½ tablespoons in a 6-inch iron), close and squeeze handles together. Turn iron and scrape off any batter that flows out.

Bake, turning every 20 seconds, until cookie is light golden brown. Open the iron to check doneness. Quickly lift out cookie with a fork or spatula; return iron to heat. Let cookies cool flat on wire racks or shape in a cone while still hot and pliable, then cool. Store in airtight containers for up to a week at room temperature; freeze for longer storage. Serve plain or fill just before serving with whipped cream. Makes about 18 Krumkakes.

SPRITZ

1 cup real butter
⅔ cup sugar
2 cups all-purpose flour
3 egg yolks
1 teaspoon vanilla

Cream butter and sugar until light and fluffy. Blend in remaining ingredients; mix thoroughly. Press a small amount of dough at a time through a cookie press onto an ungreased baking sheet, using the plate for the shape desired. Bake at 375° for 6 to 9 minutes, until set but not brown.

Note: If desired, sprinkle with colored sugar before baking.

Makes about 5 dozen.

ROSETTES

2 eggs
1 cup all-purpose flour
1 tablespoon granulated sugar
¼ teaspoon salt
1 cup milk
Vegetable oil for deep frying
Confectioners' *or* granulated sugar

Beat eggs slightly; add flour, sugar, salt and milk and beat until smooth or mix in a blender. Place rosette iron in fat while heating to 375° on a candy thermometer. Remove iron; tap excess fat from iron. Dip hot iron into batter just to the top (do not let batter run over top of form); then dip into hot fat. The batter should peel off the iron. Fry until golden brown. Drain on absorbent paper towel. Sprinkle cookies with confectioners' or granulated sugar.

Makes 4 to 6 dozen.

A Potpourri of Recipes

BIBB OR BOSTON LETTUCE MIMOSA

"A good, hearty salad—the dressing is one of my favorites."

This is a quick salad to which you can add almost anything—cold slivered meat, julienne cheese strips, raw or cooked vegetables, cooked chicken strips. Count on using about ½ head lettuce per serving. Wash and dry your lettuce and chill. This will be the basis for the salad, and to this add:

Tomato(es), washed and thinly sliced
Chopped scallions
Slivered green pepper
Sliced celery heart

Dressing:
3 parts olive oil
1 part wine vinegar
1 teaspoon Dijon mustard (adjust to taste and amount being made)
Salt and pepper to taste
Chopped fresh parsley (optional)
Chopped scallions *or* onion (optional)
Finely chopped hard-boiled eggs, for garnish

Mix the amount of dressing you will need for the number of servings you plan. When mixing dressing, measure into a jar with a lid and shake well, or put in the blender. Or, if using a whisk, mix the mustard, vinegar, salt and pepper together; whisk the oil in a bit at a time. It should become thick, but will not stay that way. Add optional parsley and onion.

To serve, pour dressing over greens and vegetables and then sprinkle finely chopped hard-boiled eggs over the whole salad.

Serves as many as desired

VEGETABLE FRITTATA

"When you're tired of preparing vegetables the same old way, try this recipe. It combines several vegetables into one tasty dish.

1 cup sliced fresh mushrooms
⅔ cup chopped onion
⅔ cup chopped green *or* red pepper
1½ cups chopped zucchini, unpeeled
3 cloves garlic, minced
3 tablespoons olive oil
Salt and pepper to taste
6 eggs, beaten
½ cup half-and-half
4 tablespoons dry vermouth
½ teaspoon salt
Dash freshly ground black pepper
1 cup soft bread cubes
1 8-ounce package cream cheese, cubed
1½ cups shredded Cheddar cheese

Sauté the vegetables in olive oil until just crisp. Sprinkle with salt and pepper. Remove from heat. Beat the eggs, adding half-and-half, vermouth, salt and pepper to taste. Add vegetable mixture and bread cubes. Fold in the cubed cream cheese carefully so cubes remain intact. Pour into a well-greased 8x12-inch oven-proof baking pan. Sprinkle top with Cheddar cheese. Bake for 30 to 40 minutes in 350° oven, until just firm. Let rest 10 minutes before serving.

Serves 6

PEACH MELBA PLUS

"Peaches, raspberries, ice cream and whipped cream . . . a pretty combination but do not serve after a heavy meal."

8 fresh or canned peach halves
8 scoops vanilla ice cream
1 cup heavy cream, whipped
½ cup slivered toasted almonds

Melba sauce:

½ cup red currant jelly
½ cup sugar
1 cup pulp and juice of raspberries (fresh or frozen)
½ tablespoon arrowroot *or* cornstarch
1 tablespoon cold water

If peaches are fresh, peel and cut in half. Make a syrup by boiling 2 cups sugar with 1 cup water. Add peaches and poach them for 10 to 15 minutes or until they are tender. **If peaches are canned,** melt 3 tablespoons firmly packed brown sugar in 3 tablespoons peach juice and sauté peaches for 10 minutes. Sprinkle with a little fresh lemon juice and sauté another 2 minutes. Refrigerate.

For sauce, add jelly and sugar to raspberries. (If using frozen, sweetened raspberries, omit the sugar.) Bring to boiling point. Mix arrowroot or cornstarch with cold water and stir into mixture. Cook until thick and clear. Strain raspberries through sieve by pressing with back of spoon to remove seeds.

To serve: In each dessert glass, place a peach half and fill with a scoop of ice cream. Spoon some of the raspberry sauce over the ice cream. Top this with a tablespoon of whipped cream and sprinkling of toasted almonds.

Serves 8

SCALLOPED OYSTERS

"I am not too fond of raw oysters, but this dish is a favorite of mine. It is rich, so a little goes a long way."

- 1 pint fresh oysters
- 2 cups medium coarse cracker crumbs
- ½ cup butter *or* margarine, melted
- Pepper to taste
- ¾ cup half-and-half
- ¼ cup oyster liquor
- ½ teaspoon salt
- ¼ teaspoon Worcestershire sauce
- Squeeze of fresh lemon juice

Drain oysters, removing any shell pieces, and reserve ¼ cup liquor. Combine cracker crumbs and melted butter or margarine. Spread ⅓ of the crumb mixture in a greased, 8x1½-inch round pan, or in 6 individual shells if used for an appetizer. Cover with ½ the oysters and sprinkle with pepper. Using another ⅓ of the crumbs, spread a second layer and cover with remaining oysters and sprinkle of pepper. Combine half-and-half, reserved oyster liquor, salt, Worcestershire sauce and squeeze of lemon juice. Pour over oysters. Top with remaining crumbs. Bake in 350° oven about 40 minutes.

Serves 4 for the main course or 6 as an appetizer.

PEPPERED STEAK

"A dish that should be prepared for a small intimate party, so you can ask your guests to come to the kitchen to see the fireworks!"

- 4 1½-inch-thick slices of filet of beef
- Cracked black pepper
- 4 tablespoons butter *or* margarine
- ½ cup mango chutney, finely chopped and heated
- ¼ cup brandy

Press the cracked black pepper into the filets with the palm of your hand so it will stick. Use the amount you like. Melt butter or margarine in heavy skillet and when good and hot, add filets and sauté to desired doneness. Spread each steak with 2 tablespoons heated chutney. Pour brandy over meat in skillet. Light the brandy and watch the flames!

Note: Depending on the brandy, this can be spectacular, so be handy with a lid to control flame.

Serves 4

TUNA-SHRIMP AU GRATIN

"A tasty yet inexpensive dish for a ladies' luncheon."

2 tablespoons butter *or* margarine
⅔ cup chopped onion
½ cup chopped green pepper
½ cup chopped red bell pepper *or* ¼ cup canned pimiento
½ cup chopped celery
2 7-ounce cans white tuna, drained and flaked
½ pound tiny Alaskan shrimp
2 teaspoons fresh lemon juice
1 cup real mayonnaise

Topping:
½ cup fine dry bread crumbs
⅓ cup grated Parmesan cheese
2 tablespoons butter *or* margarine, melted

In medium-size skillet, melt the butter or margarine and sauté onions, peppers and celery for about 10 minutes, stirring from time to time. Add the tuna (in medium chunks), shrimp and lemon juice; mix well and heat through. Remove from heat. Add mayonnaise and mix, without breaking up too much. Spoon into individual, small shallow serving shells or dishes, or into a 1-quart, buttered oven casserole. Top with mixture of crumbs, Parmesan cheese and melted butter or margarine. Bake for 20 minutes or until hot and bubbly, in a 350° oven.
Serves 6

SAUSAGE STRATA

"I like this for an easy brunch or a Sunday supper."

1 pound bulk pork sausage, mild *or* hot, according to taste
1 teaspoon dry mustard
6 slices white bread with crusts removed
1 cup grated mild Cheddar *or* American cheese
3 eggs, slightly beaten
1¼ cups milk
¾ cup half-and-half
1 teaspoon Worcestershire sauce
½ teaspoon salt
Dash pepper
2 canned green chilies, seeded and chopped

Cook sausage and drain off fat, then stir in the mustard. Arrange bread in an 8x13-inch buttered pan. Put sausage and cheese on top of the bread. Mix eggs, milk, half-and-half, Worcestershire sauce, salt and pepper. Pour egg mixture over sausage and cheese. Let set, refrigerated, about 3 hours or more, even overnight.

To serve, sprinkle with the chopped chilies and a little extra grated cheese over the top. Bake at 350°, covered, for 30 minutes or until set, then remove cover for a few minutes to brown.

Note: More green chilies may be added according to your taste.
Serves 4

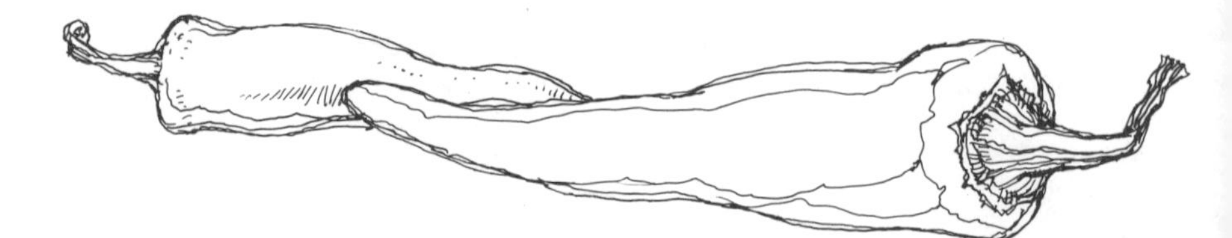

WHIPPED LEMON DRESSING

"A delicious dressing for fresh fruits or any kind of mixed canned fruits."

½ cup mayonnaise
½ cup heavy cream
¼ cup fresh lemon juice
2 to 3 drops Tabasco® pepper sauce
Few drops Worcestershire sauce
¼ cup dry vermouth
¼ cup dairy sour cream
Rind of 1 lemon, finely grated
Salt and pepper to taste
Chopped fresh parsley (optional)

Mix all ingredients together and let set in refrigerator for ½ hour or more before serving. Chopped parsley may be added for color.

Makes about 1½ cups

CHICKEN VIENNA

"Chicken, vegetables, wine and sour cream cooked together for a tasty combination."

⅓ cup olive oil
1 3½- to 4-pound frying chicken, cut into serving pieces
All-purpose flour
Salt and pepper
1 large onion, chopped
2 cloves garlic, chopped
¾ pound fresh mushrooms, sliced
2 large fresh tomatoes, peeled, seeded and chopped
1 tablespoon fresh chopped cilantro *or* 1 teaspoon dried tarragon, crushed
½ cup dry vermouth
1 tablespoon all-purpose flour
¾ cup dairy sour cream

In a large skillet, heat olive oil and brown pieces of chicken which have been rolled in mixture of flour, salt and pepper. Remove pieces of chicken as they brown and put aside. Into same skillet, add chopped onion and garlic; sauté for 4 minutes. Add mushrooms; sauté for 3 minutes then add tomatoes. Over this sprinkle cilantro or tarragon, then add vermouth and mix well. Simmer for 3 minutes. Put chicken into skillet and spoon some of the vegetable mixture over pieces. Cover skillet tightly and simmer for 30 minutes, basting the chicken twice during this period with sauce. Remove chicken from skillet.

Sprinkle 1 tablespoon flour over sauce in skillet and stirring with whisk, simmer for 5 minutes until sauce thickens. Add the sour cream and return chicken to skillet. Heat gently for 4 to 5 minutes. Remove chicken to heated platter. Check sauce for seasoning. Spoon sauce over chicken and serve with rice.

Serves 4 to 6

SAVORY CHICKEN BAKE

"Sometimes we all have guests who can't eat spicy food. This is a mild flavored casserole but very good."

- 4 cups finely chopped cooked chicken
- 3 cups soft bread crumbs
- 2 cups cooked long-grain white rice
- ¾ cup chopped onion
- ¾ cup chopped celery
- 1 4-ounce jar pimiento, drained and chopped
- ¾ teaspoon salt
- ¾ teaspoon poultry seasoning
- 1½ cups chicken broth
- 1½ cups milk
- ⅔ cup sliced toasted almonds *or* sliced water chestnuts (optional)
- 4 eggs, slightly beaten

Rich mushroom sauce:

- 1 10½-ounce can cream of mushroom soup
- 1 cup dairy sour cream
- 1 4-ounce can mushrooms, undrained

Combine all ingredients. Spoon into 13x9x3-inch baking dish. Bake in 350° oven until knife inserted comes out clean, about 50 to 55 minutes. Cut in squares.

For sauce, combine all ingredients in saucepan and heat, stirring until thoroughly blended. For a special occasion, drain juice from mushrooms and substitute ¼ cup dry sherry for the liquid.

Serves 10 to 12

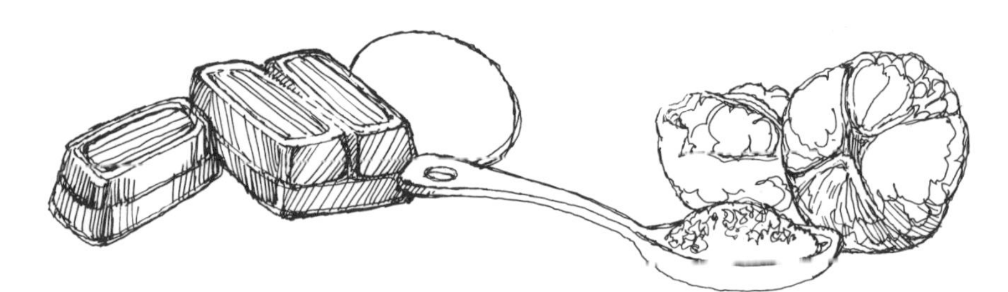

FRENCH SILK PIE

"A luscious melt-in-your-mouth pie. Don't serve large pieces because it is very, very rich."

For shell, spread pie plate lavishly with butter or margarine, as thick as you can get it. Press shredded coconut into butter until surface is coated with a thick layer. Bake at 300° until golden, approximately 20 minutes. Cool and chill.

Filling:

- 1 cup butter *or* margarine
- 1 cup sugar
- 2 eggs
- 2 ounces bitter chocolate, melted and cooled
- 1½ tablespoons brandy *or* rum
- 2 tablespoons instant coffee
- ½ cup coarsely chopped walnuts

For filling, cream butter or margarine and sugar. Add eggs, 1 at a time, beating at least 3 minutes after addition of each egg. Mixture should be very thick and smooth. Stir in chocolate, brandy or rum, coffee and nuts. Turn into shell and chill.

Serves 8

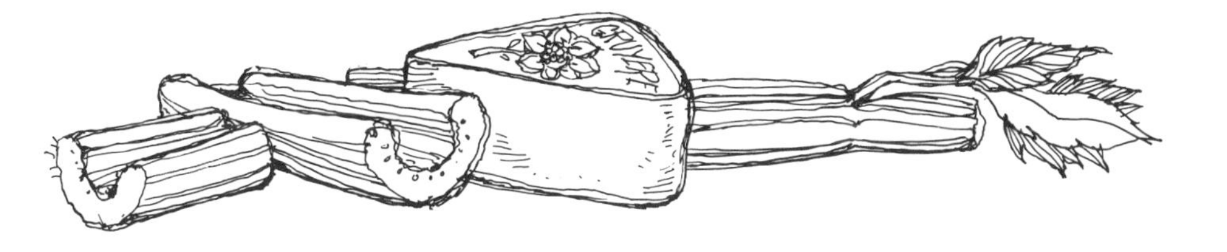

CELERY AU GRATIN

"Delicious with lamb or pork."

6 tablespoons butter *or* margarine
1 teaspoon salt
½ teaspoon freshly ground black pepper
1 large bunch of celery, trimmed and cut into 1-inch-thick slices
¾ cup grated Gruyere cheese
Freshly ground black pepper
½ cup bread crumbs
2 tablespoons butter *or* margarine, melted

In large skillet, melt 6 tablespoons butter or margarine with salt and pepper; add the celery and turn until well coated. Cook covered, tossing from time to time until just tender. Butter well a 1-quart baking dish. Transfer celery to dish and cover with the grated cheese and another grind of pepper. Toss bread crumbs in about 2 tablespoons melted butter or margarine; sprinkle overall. Bake at 375° until cheese melts and the crumbs are browned.

Serves 4 to 6

SWEET AND SOUR MEATBALLS

"Good for an hors d'oeuvre as well as an entrée. Delicious served with rice."

Meatballs:
1 egg, beaten
1 cup soft bread crumbs
2 tablespoons chopped onion
2 tablespoons milk
¾ teaspoon salt
1 pound ground beef
2 tablespoons vegetable oil

Sauce:
1 8¾-ounce can pineapple tidbits, reserve syrup
¼ cup firmly packed brown sugar
2 tablespoons cornstarch
½ cup water
¼ cup cider vinegar
1 tablespoon soy sauce
1 5-ounce can water chestnuts, thinly sliced
1 green pepper, cut in strips

For meatballs, combine egg, bread crumbs, onion, milk and salt. Add the ground beef and mix well. Shape into 24 1-inch balls. In large skillet, brown meatballs in hot vegetable oil. Drain off fat.

For sauce, drain pineapple, reserving syrup. In medium-size saucepan, combine brown sugar and cornstarch. Blend in reserved syrup, water, vinegar and soy sauce. Cook and stir over low heat until thickened and bubbly. Drain and thinly slice water chestnuts. Stir chestnuts, meatballs, green pepper and pineapple into sauce mixture. Heat to boiling. Serve with rice.

Serves 4 to 6

TIA JUANA SKILLET

"A good family dish. Serve with a green salad."

- 1 pound bulk pork sausage
- ½ pound ground beef
- ¾ cup chopped onion
- ¾ cup chopped green pepper
- 2 tablespoons sugar
- 1 teaspoon salt
- 1 tablespoon chili powder
- 1 1-pound can tomatoes
- 1 8-ounce can tomato sauce
- 1½ cups shell macaroni
- 1 cup dairy sour cream
- Grated Parmesan cheese (optional)

Brown meat and drain off excess fat. Add onion and green pepper; sauté until tender but not brown. Stir in sugar, salt, chili powder, tomatoes, tomato sauce and cover. Simmer about 25 minutes. Cook shell macaroni 3 minutes less than package instructions, so it is barely tender. Stir shells and sour cream into meat mixture. Continue cooking for 15 minutes. If desired, serve with grated Parmesan cheese.

Serves 6

FILET OF FLOUNDER AU GRATIN

"Here's a 'dress up' sauce for an inexpensive fish."

- 6 frozen flounder filets, thawed
- Salt and pepper
- ½ cup chopped fresh parsley
- 2 tablespoons butter *or* margarine
- 2 tablespoons fresh lemon juice
- ½ pound fresh mushrooms, sliced
- 1 tablespoon all-purpose flour
- 1½ cups heavy cream
- 2 tablespoons sherry
- 2 tablespoons grated Parmesan cheese
- 1 tablespoon seasoned bread crumbs
- Paprika

Dry fish and arrange in shallow baking pan, sprinkle with salt, pepper and parsley. Preheat oven to 475°. Melt butter or margarine in saucepan; pour in lemon juice. Add mushrooms and sauté over low heat 5 to 10 minutes, stirring occasionally. Stir in flour. Add cream and stir until thick. Simmer over very low heat 5 minutes. Add sherry. Taste for seasoning and blend well. Pour sauce over fish. Sprinkle with cheese, bread crumbs and paprika. Bake in lower half of oven for 20 minutes, or until top is browned and fish flakes easily with a fork. Serve immediately.

Serves 6

CHILI
POWDER
M.K. Howe

Date: ______________ Time: ______________

GUESTS	

MENU	

NOTES

Date: ____________

Time: ____________

GUESTS	

MENU	

NOTES

Date: ______________ Time: ______________

GUESTS	

MENU	

NOTES

Date: ________________ Time: ________________

GUESTS

MENU

NOTES

Date: ______________ Time: ______________

GUESTS	

MENU	

NOTES

Date: ______________ Time: ______________

GUESTS	

MENU	

NOTES

Date: ________________ Time: ________________

GUESTS

MENU

NOTES

Date: ____________ Time: ____________

GUESTS	
MENU	
NOTES	

Date: ____________ Time: ____________

GUESTS	

MENU	

NOTES

Date: ____________________ Time: ____________________

GUESTS

MENU

NOTES

Date: ________________ Time: ________________

GUESTS

MENU

NOTES

Recipe Index

APPETIZERS

"Many entrées and appetizers are interchangeable — the only difference being — serve smaller portions for appetizers."

BEEF

BREADS AND BISCUITS

BREAD AND BISCUITS (con't.)

CASSEROLES

CHEESE AND EGG

COOKIES

CREPES AND PANCAKES

DESSERTS

FRUITS AND SALADS

FRUITS AND SALADS (con't.)

LAMB

PASTA

PIES

PORK

POULTRY

POULTRY (con't.)

SAUCES, SALAD DRESSINGS AND DIPS

SEAFOOD

SOUPS (HOT AND COLD)

VEGETABLES

Born and raised in Topeka, Kansas, **MIRIAM BAKER LOO** is an accomplished and creative homemaker who has been an enthusiastic cook since her youth. After graduation from Washburn University of Topeka, Kansas, she was married to Orin Loo. In addition to raising three sons, with her husband, in 1950 she founded Current, Inc., a national mail order firm located in Colorado Springs. The company has grown from a basement business whose first product lines included Post-A-Notes and recipe cards designed by Mr. Loo to a thriving enterprise serving millions of customers today.

A participant in many gourmet food classes, Miriam Loo has been responsible for the many recipes for notes, calendars and personal enclosures in the Current product line for several years.

Long involved in volunteer activities, Miriam Loo has received national recognition for her accomplishments in community work, church leadership and business.